AUTHORS NOTES

Writing this book has been one of the most emotion⌐ my life. Looking back on everything I have been through—every challenge, every heartbreak, and every moment I thought I wouldn't survive—has reminded me of just how strong I really am. This story is deeply personal, and while I have shared so much, I also made the decision to keep certain details to myself. Some memories are too painful, some involve others whose stories are not mine to tell, and some have simply faded over time.

You may notice that I have not included any names in this book. That choice was intentional. I wanted to keep this story focused on me—my journey, my emotions, my growth. While so many people have shaped my life, this book is about my experience, and I wanted to tell it in a way that felt true to me.

There was so much more I could have written, but I had to draw a line between what was my story to share and what belonged to others. Some events have been watered down—not to hide the truth, but to protect myself and my own peace. Even so, every word on these pages is real, raw, and honest.

I hope that in reading this, someone out there feels less alone. Maybe you've had a difficult childhood, faced struggles that felt impossible to overcome, or questioned if you'd ever find happiness. If that's you, I want you to know that there is always hope. Life can be cruel and unfair, but it can also be beautiful. I have found love, I have found purpose, and most importantly, I have found myself.

To those who have supported me—whether in the past, present, or through simply reading my words—thank you. This book may be my story, but it is also a testament to survival, resilience, and the power of never giving up.

If I can make it through, so can you.

CHAPTER 1

From my earliest memories of my childhood, I could only recall the dark moments, the moments that left scars in places that no one could see. My mother, though she had her own reasons for the way she treated me, made it clear that love was not something I could count on.

If I ate at school, dinner at home was forbidden. If I wet the bed, it was not just an accident-it was something to be ashamed of, something that made me feel small. I would be sent to school in a nappy, as though the world needed to see how 'broken' I was.

The worst came one day when I had an accident in my underwear. Instead of compassion, I was met with cruelty. Soap forced into my mouth. It was supposed to teach me a lesson, but all it did was teach me that no matter what I did, it was never enough to escape the hurt.

There were moments – brief flashes – where I thought maybe just maybe my mom cared about me. One such moment was when she asked me to take some cardboard boxes outside. I was so small I couldn't reach the door latch. When I asked for help, she did not just open the door – she snapped. The anger in her voice made me shrink inside, and I tried not to make it worse. As she swung the door open, I squeezed through, desperate to get the job done and avoid any more conflict. But in my attempt to rush I grabbed the door frame swinging myself out of the way to toss the boxes into the alley. In the chaos I didn't realize what was happening until it was all too late.

The door slammed shut.

The pain was immediate and unbearable. I screamed, my throat burning as the hinges of the door crushed my fingers. I don't remember much of what happened next, except the cold rush of panic and the sting of tears in my eyes. I was taken to the hospital, my fingers throbbing, blood staining the fabric of my clothes.

And then something strange happened.

My mom, who had been so cold and harsh, cried. She held me, and for the first time in what felt like forever, I felt loved – like she actually cared. I needed her to care, and for that brief moment, I let myself believe she did.

I had to get stitches in my one finger, but the doctor said I would be okay. We were told to go back for a follow up appointment in a few days.

But that never happened.

Mom had plans.

At around the age of 6 my dad and my stepmom fought for custody. It felt like a lifeline at first, a chance for something different. But as soon as I stepped into my new life, it became clear that I still did not belong. I was an outsider in a house full of unfamiliar faces. My stepsisters and my half-sister, though family, felt like strangers. The tension was thick, and I didn't know how to deal with it.

So, I rebelled. I fought against rules and lashed out at my stepmom, hoping to be seen, hoping to be understood. But the more I pushed. The more I pushed away. So, at the age of only 12 both my dad and stepmom made a decision that would change everything.

They sent me to respite care, a children's home where I was meant to be safe. The children's home was a strange place, full of children who had their own stories of pain and loss. I wasn't the only one trying to make sense of the world, but that didn't make it any easier. I had no idea where I fitted in.

The days blurred together, and I felt lost in the system, just another kid who didn't have the answers to the questions everyone kept asking me. But despite all the chaos there was a small spark of hope I didn't know then, but that spark would become my driving force – the hope that one day I would find my place in the world, where I could finally heal.

CHAPTER 2

The children's home was only a short walk from my dad and stepmom's house, just 0.2 miles—a six-minute stroll that felt like a lifetime. But no matter how close I was, it might as well have been on the other side of the world. I'd visit on Wednesdays and Sundays. Wednesdays were simple—after school, I'd walk back to their house for tea. But Sundays… Sundays were for church. I would sit there with my stepsisters and half-sister, trying to focus on the hymns, but my mind would always drift. I could hear the sounds of my dad's voice, the rustling of my sisters beside me. But I wasn't really there. The house I had left behind, the one that had never felt like home, would always be with me in the pit of my stomach. Slowly, the visits became less frequent. It was like the ties were being loosened one by one, and I couldn't stop the unravelling.

The children's home became my new reality. A place where rules were strict, and the staff barely knew how to deal with a kid like me. I didn't fit in with the other kids; I was too angry, too defiant. My fists were always clenched, ready to lash out at anyone who looked at me the wrong way. And it wasn't just the other kids—staff were targets too. I would pick fights with anyone who dared to try and control me. One day, a cleaner came into my room and knocked one of my favourite teddy ornaments off the shelf. It shattered on the floor, and something inside me snapped. I knew she had done it, and she kept denying it. I screamed at her, shouted until my voice cracked. "You broke it!" I yelled. She just stood there, claiming she did not, but it was her, no one else had been in my room. I went at her, not caring about anything other than my rage. She started crying. I didn't care. The next day, I was told she had retired. The staff made it sound like she had chosen to leave, but I knew better. I had broken her, and I did not feel bad about it.

One day, I pushed a staff member down two little steps in the house—nothing too big, just a small flight of steps leading down to the back door. He hurt his back and had to take six weeks off work. I didn't even know why I did it. There was no particular reason, nothing that triggered it—just this overwhelming urge to act out. I could still hear the thud when he hit the floor. The staff member never looked at me the same after that, and I knew I had taken things too far. But it did not stop me. I was spiralling, and I didn't know how to stop.

There was one kid, another girl who came to the home around the same time I did. You would think we would have been able to bond—same age, same experience, but we could not have been more different. She was the type of girl who needed to be the centre of attention, who strutted around like she owned the place. I was not going to bow to her, no matter how hard she tried to make me. One afternoon, I was sitting on the floor in the living room, painting my toenails while I watched TV. I was lost in the moment, trying to ignore the chaos around me. Then, without warning, she came up behind me, shoving me so hard that my nail polish went flying everywhere, covering my feet and the carpet. Before I knew it, her hands were hitting me, and we were tearing into each other like animals. We fought until we were both gasping for air, until the staff had to separate us. I hated her, but when she left the home a few months later, I was relieved. The atmosphere felt lighter without her there, like I could breathe again. But life has a funny way of messing with you. She came back—a good few months after she left. And this time, I didn't have my own room anymore. We had to share. She seemed different, more grown up, and strangely, we didn't fight as often. But that didn't mean we got along. The tension still lingered, just beneath the surface. She was still the same person, and so was I. The constant competition between us never fully disappeared.

There is one memory that stands out from that time. Two other kids in the home approached me one afternoon and asked if I wanted to smoke with them. Not cigarettes, but something that I would call — wacky backy. I didn't want to be left out. I wanted to fit in, to be one of them, so I agreed. We went to the big Mulberry tree in the garden, hiding behind its thick branches like we were doing something dangerous. I tried to act cool, rolling my own, even though I didn't really know what I was doing. The moment I lit it; I coughed so hard that my throat burned. I couldn't stop though. I had to prove I could handle it. I puffed away until I could not breathe. The world started spinning. I didn't know what was happening, but the next thing I remember, I was lying in the bathroom, unable to move. My body was paralyzed, and all I could hear were voices—people shouting my name, panicking. One of the kids I had smoked with was crying, thinking she had killed me. I felt like I was sinking into the floor, a heavy weight pressing down on me. Then, someone burst through the door—a staff member, I think. They scooped me up, splashing water in my face, trying to wake me up. "Don't ever do that again," they whispered, holding me tight. I never did. That was the last time I tried to be cool.

Despite the chaos of the children's home, there was one bright spot I could always count on: meeting my best friend. She lived just at the top of the road, barely a five-minute walk from the home. I would see her on my walks to and from school, or sometimes when I went to the shops. We didn't start off as friends, though. In fact, we did not like each other at first. Both of us thought the other was a bit… bitchy.

Looking back, I think we were both just defensive—two girls who were used to keeping our guard up. But somehow, despite that initial coolness, something clicked between us. We started talking, and slowly, over time, we found common ground. Before I knew it, I was spending all my free time at her house. We would hang out for hours, playing games like Dream Phone, gossiping, and, of course, sneaking out to go smoke—cigarettes this time—at the top of Moneywise car park. It was a little reckless, a little rebellious, but in those moments, I felt alive, like I was finally living. If I ever walked out of the children's home without telling anyone, the staff knew exactly where I would be. I'd be at her house, and they were more than okay with that. Her parents welcomed me like I was one of their own. They didn't judge me for what I had been through or where I came from. They just loved having me around. Her dad was always making me laugh, cracking jokes that made everything feel lighter. And her mom… she worried about everything. If we were going out, she would make sure we had everything we needed—snacks, jackets, anything to make sure we were safe and warm. It was strange, in the best way. It was the first time I had ever really felt like I was wanted somewhere. Like I was a part of a family.

They weren't perfect, of course. No family is. But her parents loved their children, and they loved me too. And for the first time in a long time, I felt like I belonged somewhere. They made me smile in a way I hadn't in years, and when I was with them, I could forget about the chaos of the children's home, even if only for a little while.

CHAPTER 3

Two years passed in the children's home. Time blurred together with the routine of school, visits to my best friend's house, and the occasional flare-up with staff or other kids. I had my moments of peace, but there was always that underlying tension, the knowledge that I didn't truly belong there either. The visits to my dad and stepmoms had faded over time. What had once been weekly trips to see them on Sundays and Wednesdays slowly turned into something else. I wasn't going back home as much. It became clear that my dad and stepmom just couldn't see how I would fit back into their lives. They couldn't figure out how to make things work with me in their home anymore. It was like the space I had once occupied there had shifted, and it wasn't mine anymore. The idea of respite care, of just spending short times away, was no longer enough. It was becoming permanent. And then, the word "foster care" started to come up in conversations. I didn't fully understand it at first, or what it would mean for me. But I knew it wasn't just a possibility—it was becoming a reality. The staff talked about it like it was something that needed to happen, and I could see the uncertainty in my dad's eyes when the subject came up. It was clear that he and my stepmom didn't know what else to do with me. I was no longer the child they thought they could raise. I had outgrown their vision of who I should be, and I didn't know how to fit back into that. Foster care felt like the final step in the long, slow process of becoming an outsider in my own family. It was the door that closed on my life as I had known it. The one I had fought to hold onto. The one that was slipping further away with every passing day.

Moving into another home, I was filled with anxiety. The fear of not fitting in, of being unwanted, gnawed at me. But when I stepped into my new room, all of that momentarily faded. It was beautiful—fitted wardrobes, a built-in bed, and even a fold-out desk on the wall. It felt warm, cozy, and, most importantly, mine.

Christmas was right around the corner, and I wasn't sure what to expect. Would I be ignored? Would I even get a single gift? But when I woke up on Christmas morning and followed my foster mom and foster brothers into the living room, I was stunned. Three enormous piles of presents sat before us—one for each of us. I couldn't believe my eyes. Why would someone who barely knew me go out of their way to buy me anything? The details of most of the gifts are a blur, but one stood out—a brand-new TV, perfect for my perfect little space.

I settled in quickly with my foster brothers. Despite being the oldest, they never made me feel out of place. We bonded over shared experiences, one of which was taking turns on the family computer. Back then, the internet was dial-up, meaning if you were online, the house phone was out of service. I loved logging in, playing games with people from all over the world, and escaping into a reality where no one knew my past. It felt freeing.

My foster mom showed kindness in ways that weren't grand gestures but meant everything to me. Every morning, a warm croissant and a glass of orange juice waited for me in the kitchen. I could have easily made my own breakfast—I was 14, after all—but this small act made me feel cared for. It was a love I wasn't used to, and I soaked it in.

School, on the other hand, was a battlefield. The stigma of being a kid in care followed me like a shadow. Insults were thrown casually, and I constantly had my guard up. Most of the time, I ignored them, but one day in drama class, someone pushed too far. They said something about my mom, and before I even registered what was happening, I had picked up a chair and hurled it at them. A fight broke out, and while their punches barely grazed me, mine landed with force—until the teacher stepped in and separated us.

The next thing I knew, I was sitting in the headteacher's office with my foster mom, awaiting my fate. I was convinced this was the end—I'd be expelled, thrown out of school just like so many other places before. And at first, that's exactly what happened. But then, a week later, another meeting was called. My teachers advocated for me. They believed I deserved another chance. For the first time, it felt like people actually cared about my future, and that feeling stayed with me.

Not long after, I started hanging out with a new girl at school. She was bold, confident, and carried herself as though she owned the world. I admired that. She dressed older than she was, wore heavy makeup, and radiated a sense of freedom that I longed for. So, I followed her lead.

I stopped following the rules at home. I never told my foster mom where I was going, never asked if I could bring friends over—I just did whatever I pleased. She warned me multiple times, but I ignored her. Then, one night, I stayed at my friend's house without telling anyone. I knew it was wrong, but I did it anyway. And to make matters worse, I waltzed back home the next day with that same friend in tow, acting like nothing had happened.

That was the final straw. My foster mom had had enough. My bags were packed, and just like that, I was being moved again. This time, back to a children's home. Not the one I had been in before—a completely new place in an entirely different area.

As I watched my belongings being packed up, a painful realization settled in. I had done this to myself. If only I had listened. If only I had tried harder. My heart broke as I left, knowing I had lost a home where, for the first time in a long time, I had started to feel like I belonged.

Moving into the new children's home felt like stepping into a completely different world. The house was beautiful, surrounded by open space with a massive park right next door. At first, I thought I'd lucked out—it seemed quiet, almost peaceful. But reality quickly set in. This home wasn't just about having a roof over my head; it was about learning to stand on my own two feet.

At nearly 16, I was one of the oldest there, which meant more responsibilities. Unlike the younger kids, who had their meals cooked and their laundry done for them, I had to do everything myself—washing, cooking, budgeting. I had my own room, which was great, and even a little kitchen next door. On the surface, it felt like a taste of adulthood, but in reality, it was overwhelming. Balancing all of this while preparing for my GCSEs was stressful, but I was determined not to be another statistic—just another kid in care who dropped out or failed their exams.

This place was different from the last children's home. There were no fights, no constant drama. Not that I was best friends with everyone, but I had grown up enough to pick my battles. The staff were pretty cool, and one of them even used to plait my hair, which I loved. I also clicked with one of the other kids there—we spent hours making up dance routines and would perform them for the staff and other kids. It was silly but fun, and for the first time in a long while, I actually enjoyed where I was.

As part of my transition to adulthood, I had to do a four-week placement in an independent living facility. It was a huge step—living alone in my own flat, with staff only next door in an office. The idea of it scared me, especially because it happened right when my exams were in full swing. One night, I had friends over, and the next morning, I was in such a rush to get to school that I nearly missed my science exam. I managed to get there, but exhaustion hit me hard—I barely got through the questions before I actually fell asleep in the middle of the exam. Not exactly my proudest moment.

In the end, I didn't completely fail my GCSEs, but I knew I could've done better. And as for the independent living placement? I failed that. So, back to the children's home I went, at least until a new plan was put in place. Eventually, I was told I'd be moving into an independent living home—something similar to foster care, but instead of being treated as part of the family, I'd be more like a lodger.

This time, the move didn't feel as daunting. I already knew one of the girls living there from my first children's home (not the one I used to fight with), which made settling in easier. The woman running the house was kind and genuinely wanted to help. She even tried to get me to quit smoking, making me a deal—if I stopped, she'd get me tickets to see Robbie Williams at Knebworth Stadium. I was obsessed with him, so I agreed. And I actually did it—I quit. True to her word, she got me the tickets, and I was beyond excited.

But, as always, I managed to ruin things. I made the mistake of inviting some so-called friends over, and they ended up stealing from the family. That was it—I was out. I was furious—at them, at myself, at the endless cycle of screwing up and losing the good things I had. But anger didn't change the fact that I was now homeless. No amount of apologies could fix it.

This time, I had no choice but to get my act together. Next stop: a hostel.

CHAPTER 4

She was a staff member at my school, but from the moment I met her, I knew she was different. It was her first day at my school, and as soon as we spoke, she told me I reminded her of herself. She had grown up in the system too—she understood. For the first time, I felt like someone truly saw me, not just as another kid in care, but as a person with a future.

At first, she was just a staff member, but over time, she became so much more. She looked out for me in ways no one else had. Weekends at her house became my escape from the chaos of the children's home and the loneliness of independent living. I wasn't just a visitor—I was part of her family. Her two daughters treated me like a big sister, and for the first time in a long time, I felt like I belonged somewhere.

The bond we formed was something I had never experienced before. She wasn't just a teacher or a mentor—she became my safe place, my role model, and the person I trusted most. She made me feel valued, something I had struggled with for so long. Over time, she became more than just a friend or a guardian figure. She became my family, and I began calling her my aunty. It wasn't just a title; it was how I truly felt. She treated me like one of her own, and I loved her like family. But it wasn't just one-sided—I felt like I was there for her too. We weren't just mentor and student or even just family; we were friends. She never made me feel like a project or someone she had to fix. With her, my past didn't define me. She saw me as an equal, as a person who had value, just like her. We could talk about anything—life, struggles, and even silly things. She confided in me just as much as I did in her, and that made our bond even stronger.

She supported me in ways I didn't even realize I needed. When everything fell apart at the independent living house, she was the one who helped me pick up the pieces. She came to help me pack up my things, not just as a teacher or a mentor, but as someone who genuinely cared. She didn't let me fall through the cracks. While I was panicking about where I'd end up next, she was already making calls, ensuring I had somewhere safe to go.

By the time I walked out of that house for the last time, I wasn't stepping into the unknown alone—she had found me a hostel and made sure I had a place to stay. I wasn't just another lost kid in the system. I had someone fighting for me. And that changed everything.

I was in an intake hostel for females only. The plan was for me to stay for no more than four weeks, but it ended up being much longer—at least two months. Living there with so many other girls was difficult; it was nearly impossible to get along with everyone. One girl stood out, though. She was always out with older guys, and I ended up tagging along. At 17, I didn't realize how much older these guys were. We'd get into their cars, hang out, drink, and smoke—just carefree moments that eventually wore me down.

As time went on, I realized it was all becoming too much. I distanced myself from her and stopped going out as much. But even after I cut ties, my phone wouldn't stop ringing with calls from her or one of her male friends asking where I was. Eventually, I had to change my number just to get some space and peace.

A few weeks later, one of the girls who had moved out of the hostel helped me secure a room in another hostel where she had relocated. It felt like a fresh start, though it came with its own set of challenges. This new hostel was bigger, and there were still a lot of girls, but the difference was that it felt more private. It was like having my own little flat in a massive building, where each of us had our own separate space, which made things feel a little more manageable.

Right across from the hostel, there was a pub, and I started going there regularly with a few of the other girls. It was during one of those trips that I met a guy through one of the girls. He made me feel safe and secure, offering everything I thought I needed at the time. He knew exactly how to talk to me, how to make me feel seen.

After some time, I moved into my own flat at 19 years old. It was in a lovely area, not far from my friends or family. The flat was mine, and I could make it whatever I wanted it to be. It felt freeing. I filled the place with furniture my dad had given me—sofas, a cooker—and made the space truly my own. I also hung up all my photos, which had always been so important to me. I never wanted to miss a memory, and seeing them around the flat made it feel like a real home.

At first, I never expected things to go the way they did. I thought we had something real, something solid. But as time passed, things began to unravel, and I started receiving calls—calls from girls telling me they had been with him the night before. The first time, I thought it was a fluke, but then it kept happening. One after another, they all came forward, each claiming to have spent the night with him while I had been in the dark, thinking everything was fine.

The worst part wasn't just hearing it from these girls—it was how he treated me during it all. He'd belittle me by calling me when he was with one of them, pretending like he didn't even know he was dialling my number. It was as if he got some sick satisfaction from keeping me on the hook while playing me for a fool. It wasn't just the cheating—it was the disrespect, the way he made me feel like I was nothing. I wasn't the one he wanted, I was just someone to keep around while he did whatever he wanted with others.

The final straw came on Valentine's Day. I had called him, thinking he might do something special, but instead, another girl answered his phone. She was casual about it, like it was no big deal, and the sting of it hit me harder than anything before. That was the moment I realized I couldn't ignore the truth any longer. I had been living in this false reality, and now it was shattered.

The anger, the hurt—it was all too much. In a moment of pure frustration, I took all the clothes he'd left at my flat—his jeans, his shirts, his jackets—and I went to work on them. I didn't care how petty it might seem. I cut holes in everything, each cut a release for all the pain and betrayal I felt. When I was done, I packed all of it up neatly, like some twisted final goodbye, and when he came to visit next, I threw it all at him. It wasn't just about the clothes—it was about me taking back some control, showing him that I wasn't going to take his lies and disrespect anymore.

It wasn't long after I turned 20 that I discovered I was pregnant. It was like a cruel twist of fate. All the pain, the anger, the confusion—it became even more complicated. I didn't know what to think, or how to feel. But in that moment, it was clear: things would never be the same.

CHAPTER 5

Pregnancy was both an exciting and a challenging journey. Finding out I was having a boy filled me with joy, but the experience was far from easy. I struggled with hypertension and high blood pressure throughout, which meant frequent hospital visits. The constant back and forth added to my stress, making me believe that the very thing meant to monitor my health was actually making it worse.

The day I went into labour, I had a gut feeling that it was finally time. I begged my baby's father not to be gone too long because I just knew I would end up in the hospital by the end of the day. I went to my aunt's house, hoping for support, but no one believed me when I said I was in labour. Instead, they all went out shopping, leaving me to endure the contractions alone. Desperate, I went to a friend's house, but by the time I got there, my contractions were only a minute apart. It was undeniable now. An ambulance was called, and I was rushed to the hospital.

Labor was nothing short of awful. I had been in pain the entire day, and when I arrived at the hospital, I was 4cm dilated. But things took a frightening turn—my baby boy's heartbeat kept dipping, and the doctors were clearly worried. Seeing their concern only heightened my own fear, making it nearly impossible to breathe through my contractions properly. I tried focusing on a nurse's face for comfort, but when she left the room, I was left staring at a meaningless poster on the wall. My aunt, my friend, and my baby's father were all there, trying to hold my hands, but I was in such a bad state that nothing helped.

The doctors decided to break my waters to see if it would help my baby, but hours passed with no improvement. The situation was becoming more urgent. Finally, the doctor made the call—I needed an emergency C-section, and I would have to be put under general anaesthesia. I was absolutely petrified, but at that point, all I wanted was for the pain to stop and, more importantly, for my baby to be okay. His heartbeat wasn't stable, and that was all that mattered.

The last thing I remember was being rolled out of the delivery suite, a mask being placed over my face. Then, nothing.

When I woke up, everything had changed. I opened my eyes, and there he was—my baby boy, in my arms. The overwhelming realization hit me like a wave: "OMG, I'm a mom." It felt surreal, almost like a dream. But I knew, from that moment forward, that I was going to give my baby the best life possible. Nothing like the one I had been given.

After fully waking from the anaesthesia, I finally got to take him in—really see him, feel him, hold him close. It was amazing. I could not believe that this little life, this perfect little human, was mine. He was absolutely gorgeous, and in that moment, nothing else in the world mattered.

Waking up with my baby boy in my arms felt surreal. I could hardly believe I was finally holding him. He was so small, so fragile, but so perfect. My mind raced, the exhaustion from the past few hours hitting me like a wave. The pain of labour was fading, replaced by a sense of awe that I couldn't put into words. He was mine. I had carried him all this time, and now he was here, in my arms, real and breathing.

The room around me blurred, and all I could focus on was his tiny face. His little fingers curled around mine, and it felt like my entire life had led to this moment. I didn't care about anything else. The world could've fallen apart, and I wouldn't have noticed as long as he was there, safe and sound.

The doctors had been so worried when his heart rate kept dipping, and I couldn't forget the feeling of terror that had gripped me in the delivery suite. Every time the monitors beeped; my heart skipped a beat. But now, all I could do was marvel at him. This little boy, this tiny human, was going to be my everything. And I would do anything to make sure he never felt the pain I had known.

As I looked down at him, I couldn't help but think about how much my life had changed. There was no going back now, no running away from the responsibility. But somehow, I felt ready. I had to be. I promised myself I would give him everything I never had love, stability, safety.

The nurse came in shortly after I'd had a moment to process. She smiled warmly as she checked on us, and I could tell she'd seen this kind of miracle many times before. But for me, it was the most incredible thing I had ever experienced. She asked if I needed anything, but all I wanted was more time with him. Just a few more minutes, a few more moments to absorb the reality of what had just happened.

As the days passed, I stayed in the hospital for a little while to recover. I had a lot of time to think and reflect. I thought about my past, the things I had gone through, and how much I wanted to protect my son from that same kind of pain. I couldn't change my past, but I had the power to shape his future. And I would.

When it was time to go home, I felt a mix of excitement and fear. My baby and I would be starting this new chapter together, and the weight of responsibility was enormous. But for the first time in a long time, I felt hopeful. Maybe, just maybe, things could be different for us.

At four weeks old, my baby boy was still so tiny, so delicate. I had become somewhat used to the routine of being up with him in the night, rocking him gently in my arms, trying to settle him to sleep. It was supposed to be a peaceful moment, the quiet comfort of my child in my arms. But that night was different.

I was rocking him, humming softly to him when it happened. His little leg suddenly went limp in my arms, like a rag doll. I froze. My heart stopped. Something was wrong. My mind raced, but I couldn't make sense of it. He wasn't moving it, and he started crying—so loudly, so desperately. It wasn't the usual cry, the kind I'd gotten used to over the past few weeks. This was something else, something deeper, something that made my heart shatter in my chest. It sounded like he was in pain.

Panic gripped me, tightening around my throat, choking me. I tried to stay calm, but everything inside me screamed that something was horribly wrong. I immediately grabbed my phone, hands shaking so badly I almost couldn't dial. When I finally got through to 999, I could barely speak. My voice was thick with fear as I told them what had happened. I was certain his leg was broken. The way it went limp, the way he cried in pain, it felt undeniable. I was terrified. I couldn't stop thinking about how something was happening to him, and I wasn't sure if I could help him.

After I hung up with the operator, I didn't know what to do with myself. My thoughts were all over the place, spiralling with fear. It felt like everything was moving in slow motion. I called my aunty, my heart heavy with the weight of what was happening. The words felt impossible to say, but I told her what was going on. I needed her. I needed her reassurance.

Within minutes, she was at my door. I don't even remember her knocking; she was just there, rushing into my flat, her presence like a lifeline. She wrapped her arms around me, her voice calm, steady. She told me everything would be fine, that the ambulance was on the way and that I shouldn't worry. But I couldn't stop myself from worrying. I couldn't stop the panic from rising inside me.

In that moment, nothing felt fine. I held my son tightly, my eyes never leaving his face, my mind racing with thoughts of what could be happening to him. My hands were shaking as I cradled him, feeling his warmth, his tiny heartbeat against mine. But I wasn't fine. I wasn't sure if I ever would be again.

The ambulance arrived quickly, but every second had felt like a lifetime. The paramedics were calm, their voices gentle as they assessed my baby. They asked me questions, but I barely heard them. My mind was screaming, drowning everything else out. I just needed them to help him.

At the hospital, doctors and nurses moved around us, checking his leg, running tests. Over and over, they told me not to worry. "It's going to be okay," they said. "Try to stay calm." But how could I? My tiny, fragile baby was lying there in pain, and no one could tell me why. I wanted to believe them, to take comfort in their words, but I couldn't shake the feeling that something terrible was coming.

At one point, I sat with my dad in the hospital cafeteria, trying to process everything. He did what dads do—tried to make it all seem less scary, tried to remind me that accidents happen. He told me about the time his eldest daughter broke her arm when she was just two years old. "Babies' bones can be weak," he said, his voice steady, his words meant to be reassuring. "You can't stress yourself out too much." I nodded, listening, trying to let his words sink in. And for a minute—a single minute—I let myself breathe, let myself believe it would be okay.

But that moment of peace didn't last.

The next thing I knew, there were new faces in the room, serious voices speaking in hushed tones. My stomach dropped. Something was wrong. I could see it in the way they looked at me, in the way their words were carefully chosen. And then, like a punch to the gut, I heard the words that shattered everything:

Social services were talking about placing my sweet baby boy into temporary foster care.

I couldn't breathe. The world around me blurred as their words sank in. Foster care? My baby? No. No, they couldn't take him. This wasn't happening.

I felt like I was drowning, like I was being ripped apart from the inside. I wanted to scream, to make them see how wrong this was. But I could barely form words. The fear that had been gripping me all night turned into something else—pure, blinding terror.

I had fought my whole life to survive, to build something for myself, to be better than where I came from. And now, just like that, they were threatening to take the one thing that mattered most. My baby. My whole world.

I looked at him, so small, so innocent, and I knew one thing with absolute certainty.

I was not going to let them take him from me.

CHAPTER 6

I will never forget the moment they took my baby boy away from me.

Standing outside the hospital, I felt like my body was shutting down. My legs barely held me up, my chest ached like my heart had been ripped out, and my cries came out in choked, broken sobs. I didn't care who saw me. I didn't care if the entire world was watching. My baby was gone.

The social worker had taken him, just like that, and I was left standing there, empty and shattered. I had tried to be strong, to fight, to plead with them. But none of it mattered. Their minds were made up. They had their own version of events, and in their eyes, I was just another young mom who couldn't be trusted to care for her child. It didn't matter how much I loved him, how I had been the one who called 999, desperate to get him help. None of it mattered.

The days that followed blurred together. I barely functioned. I was supposed to be at home with my son, watching him grow, experiencing all his firsts. But instead, I was counting down the hours, the minutes, until my next visit at the contact centre.

Seeing him in that unfamiliar room, knowing I had only an hour, maybe two, before they would take him away again, was a different kind of torture. I tried to soak in every second—every tiny smile, every little sound he made. I held him as close as I could, memorizing the feel of him in my arms, the way he smelled, the way his little fingers curled around mine. But it was never enough. The moment I had to hand him back, I felt like I was breaking all over again.

Then came the news that changed everything.

My dad and stepmom could apply to foster him for me. When they told me, I felt something I hadn't felt in weeks—hope. If he was with them, I would get to see him more. He wouldn't be with strangers. He would be with family.

It was music to my ears. But it wasn't the same as having him home.

I had just moved into a two-bedroom house. I had set up his room, filled it with love, ready for him. But now, I had to wait. A full assessment had to be done. Social workers had to comb through every part of my dad and stepmom's lives, making sure they were fit to care for him. And then, the final court hearing would decide everything.

So, I waited.

I waited in an empty house that was supposed to be full of laughter and baby cries. I waited, staring at the crib that should have been occupied, the bottles that went unused, the tiny clothes folded neatly in drawers.

And with every passing day, I felt the weight of it pressing down on me. The fear. The uncertainty. The aching need to have my son back where he belonged.

I just had to hold on.

Within a month or so of my boy being in temporary foster care, we got the news—he could move in with my dad and stepmom. It was a relief, knowing he was finally out of the system and with family. Not as great as having him home with me, but it was what it was. At least I knew he was safe, loved, and surrounded by familiar faces.

I saw him every day except Wednesdays. Wednesdays were the hardest. The one day of the week where I felt completely disconnected from him, like I was missing a piece of myself. But every other day, I held him, fed him, played with him—did all the things a mother should. And yet, it wasn't enough. It was never enough.

A small court date was held, and they decided I should be allowed to have him overnight once a week—to "see if I coped." As if my ability to be a mother was ever the issue. As if I hadn't already proven how much I loved and cared for him. But I went along with it because what choice did, I have?

Each visit felt like another test, another hoop to jump through. I had some family worker come over, sitting in my home, watching me with him like I was on trial in my own life. I knew they were just doing their job, but it made my stomach turn every time. I wasn't some neglectful parent who needed monitoring. I was his **mum**, and all I wanted was to have my baby back where he belonged.

But social services didn't see it that way. They weren't trying to get my boy back to me full-time. If anything, they were trying to **stop** it from happening. No matter what I did, it felt like they were always looking for a reason to say no, always finding new obstacles to throw in my way. It didn't matter that I was doing everything right, that I had a stable home, that my son was thriving when he was with me. They had made up their minds about me before I ever had a chance to prove them wrong.

A couple of months passed, and the final court date was around the corner.

Everything I had been fighting for, all the pain, the waiting, the constant proving myself—it all came down to this. One final decision.

Would they give me my son back? Or would I be trapped in this endless cycle, always one step away from having him home?

I didn't know. And the not knowing was suffocating.

The final court date had arrived, and my nerves were completely out of control. My dad, my stepmom, my sister, and my baby boy were all there with me, and of course, my baby boy's dad. As I walked into the courtroom, I felt so small, like I didn't belong there. The hours dragged on, each one feeling longer than the last, but eventually, it came out that social services had medical evidence to prove that what happened to my boy was nothing more than a horrible accident—one that could've happened to anyone. The shocking part was that they had this evidence for three months but hadn't handed it over to anyone, keeping it to themselves.

All I could hear was them repeating that, because I was a former looked-after child, they thought I would need their supervision if my boy was to return home full-time. They also mentioned concerns about my relationship with my baby's dad, calling it unstable, and said that worried them. But then the judge spoke up, and his words were like a weight lifting off my chest. He told them it shouldn't matter what my past held; it had no bearing on how I could mother my child. As for my relationship, he made it clear that it could break down at any point, but that didn't mean it would stop me from being able to care for my son.

I looked over at my dad, and I could see tears streaming down his face. They weren't tears of sadness, though—they were tears of joy. The judge had made his decision: my boy was coming home full-time, and social services had no grounds to be involved with me anymore. I couldn't believe what I was hearing. My heart raced as I rushed out of the courtroom to my stepmom, who was holding my boy. I grabbed him in my arms, so full of emotion, and walked straight back into the courtroom to show the judge how happy we were with his decision.

It was a turning point, a moment when everything shifted. The judge's decision meant it was finally just me and my boy. No more worrying about social services, no more court battles—just us, moving forward together. I felt like I could breathe again, and for the first time, I wasn't carrying the weight of the past. It was time to focus on building a life for him, a life filled with love, security, and everything he deserved.

I wasn't going to let anything stand in our way. From that day on, it was all about us, and I was determined to give him the life I never had. We were a team, and nothing could break that bond.

CHAPTER 7

Being a mom to my boy had already changed everything in my life, but it was still a rollercoaster ride, especially with the constant tension in my relationship with his dad. We broke up, got back together, and broke up again—things were always rocky. But no matter what, I had my son, and that was my constant, my anchor. He became the centre of my world, and I was determined to give him everything I could, no matter what.

After his first birthday, I decided to book a holiday with my friend and our two boys. It was going to be a chance for us to escape, to have some fun and make memories. Originally, the plan was just for me and my friend, a break from everything. But when my boy's dad found out, he somehow meddled his way in, and much to my surprise, ended up coming along. It wasn't what I'd imagined, but I tried to make the best of it.

This was my boy's and my first time on a plane, and I'll never forget the anxiety I felt as we prepared for the 4-hour flight. My little one wasn't exactly thrilled to be stuck on my lap for hours, and I can't say I enjoyed it much either. He was so restless, and all I wanted was for him to be comfortable. But even though the journey was far from ideal, I held on to the excitement of what lay ahead. I knew that, in the end, the experience would be worth it.

And it was. Once we arrived at our destination, the holiday truly began. We made the best of the situation, even with the unexpected addition of my boy's dad. The boys were both so young but seeing them play together and explore was heartwarming. The laughter, the moments of joy - they made every ounce of stress worth it. It wasn't just a getaway; it was a chance to build memories with my son that I knew we'd both cherish forever. The feeling of being together, away from the usual pressures, was like a breath of fresh air.

One of the best moments came when we lounged by the pool. Watching my boy splash around with the other kids, laughing and smiling, was one of those rare moments when time seemed to stand still. My friend and I sat back, enjoying the sunshine and catching up, but I was fully present in watching my son. Seeing him so happy, so carefree, filled my heart with pride. This was what life was about - creating these experiences for him, moments of pure joy that I knew would shape his childhood.

When we returned home, reality set in. The weather was freezing, and the rush of the holidays hit me hard. But there was a silver lining - I realized that Christmas was just around the corner, and this year, it would be my boy's first Christmas at home with me. I couldn't wait to make it unforgettable.

I planned everything down to the smallest detail. I wanted to spoil him rotten and give him all the things I never had as a child. It wasn't about the presents; it was about showing him how much he meant to me. Taking him to see Santa was one of those things I had been dreaming about, and I couldn't wait to see his face light up. I was determined to make this Christmas perfect, something I could look back on and know that I had given him a holiday full of love and happiness.

On Christmas Day, we went to my dad and stepmoms for Christmas dinner. I was finally able to share the joy of the holiday with them, with my boy in tow. It was so special to see him surrounded by family, their smiles and warmth making the day even more magical.

But the best part of it all was seeing my boy's smile. When I looked at him, I knew everything was right. He was happy, and I was happy.

Seeing him light up over the simplest things, like the decorations and the laughter around the table, was the perfect gift. I realized in that moment that I was doing something right. For the first time in my life, I was creating the kind of memories I had always wanted - memories filled with love, laughter, and joy.

It was a reminder of how far I'd come and how much I had to give. My boy was my everything, and I was determined to be the best mom I could be for him. Christmas had never been more meaningful. It wasn't about what we had or didn't have—it was about the love we shared and the bond that was growing stronger every day. And for the first time in a long while, I felt like I was exactly where I was meant to be.

After my 23rd birthday, I was hit with a shock to the system—I found out I was pregnant again. I was on contraception, so it was a complete surprise. I had no words and didn't know what to do, feeling overwhelmed by it all. I decided to let my stepmom and dad know, so I sent them a message to break the news. When I reached out, it was such a relief to finally tell someone. And they responded with warmth, even joking about not having both kids over on the same nights. That little bit of humour helped me process things, but it was still a lot to take in. It made me laugh a little amidst the chaos, but I still had so much to process. Their response helped lighten the moment, but it was still a lot to take in.

Despite the shock, I knew I was going to move forward with the pregnancy. I was excited about the idea of giving my son a sibling and couldn't wait to see what the future held. When it came time to find out the gender, my boy's dad came with me to the appointment. I was thrilled when we were told it was another baby boy. His face lit up, and I was just as happy. I was going to be a mom of two boys, and I couldn't wait to meet him.

The preparations for my new baby boy's arrival were a mix of excitement and practicality. I was always out shopping for new things for him, but I had most of what I needed from my first son. But then, my new baby decided to come 6 weeks early, and everything changed. It happened the day before my stepsister's wedding. I started feeling contractions, and my heart dropped - I knew it was happening. I called my boy's dad first, then I called my stepmom to let her know what was going on. I remember her asking me, "Have you called the hospital?" When I said no and told her I had only called their dad, she quickly replied, "Well, he's not going to deliver the baby, is he?" It made me laugh, even though I was in pain. So, I called the hospital, and they sent an ambulance right away since my contractions were only two minutes apart.

When I got to the hospital, I was already 7cm dilated, and everything seemed to be progressing quickly. I thought things were going smoothly, but then a doctor came in and put a monitor on my belly. I could see the concern in his eyes—he was looking at something on the screen. My baby's heart rate kept stopping, and that familiar feeling of worry washed over me. They discovered the umbilical cord was wrapped around his neck. Within moments, it was decided that I would need an emergency C-section. Everything was happening so fast, and I felt a mix of fear and urgency. I just wanted my baby to be okay.

When I woke up, the first thing I saw was my dad and stepmom standing by my side. My 2-year-old son was there too, looking down at me with his baby brother in my arms. It was a surreal moment; one filled with so much love and emotion. I had two beautiful boys now, and nothing - no stress, no drama - was going to come between us. I was determined that nothing would get in the way of the love I felt for them, not even the difficulties in my relationship with their dad. My boys were my world, and together, we were going to be a family.

Watching my first son adore his new baby brother was the most beautiful sight. It made every challenge worth it.

I was ready for this new chapter with my boys—no matter what, I knew we'd make it through together. We were strong, and we had each other.

CHAPTER 8

Breaking up with their dad wasn't hard for me—it was a relief. I had known for a while that it was what I needed, and when the time came, I didn't hesitate. I wasn't conflicted or unsure; I was ready. Our relationship had reached its end, and it was time for me to step into a new chapter of my life, one where I could finally focus on myself and my boys without the weight of a relationship that no longer served us.

Everyone around me had heard the talk before—the moments of breaking up, of making up—but this time, there was no going back. I was certain. I needed to be more than just a partner and a mom. I needed to rediscover who I was as an individual, and that meant creating a life where I could finally breathe and grow.

Not long after, I moved into a new home. It was a fresh start, and I couldn't have been more excited. A 3-bedroom house—one for each of my boys and one for me. My youngest was just 8 months old, and while it felt like a big step, it was exactly what we needed. The house felt like our space, our sanctuary. It was a place where we could be ourselves, a place where we could start over and make new memories, away from the past.

For the first time, I truly felt like I was creating something just for us—a home where my boys could thrive, and where I could be myself without any distractions. It was empowering to know that I was the one making this happen. The house wasn't just a roof over our heads; it was a symbol of my independence and my commitment to our future. This was our time, and I was ready to make the most of it.

As I settled into my new life with my boys, I started to realize just how much I had lost myself in the past. Being in a relationship for so long, I had forgotten what it was like to just be me. But now, as a single mother, I had the chance to reclaim that. I loved the freedom I felt—no more worrying about someone else's moods or expectations. For the first time in a long time, I didn't have to navigate someone else's world; I could focus on mine and my boys.

I was living life on my terms. I had the space to figure out who I was outside of being a partner and a mother. I found myself surrounded by people who genuinely cared about me and my boys—friends, family, and even new faces who just wanted to see us happy. Their support was overwhelming in the best way possible. They celebrated my independence, cheered on my journey, and made me feel like I could take on anything. It was a beautiful feeling, being surrounded by love and positivity, knowing that people genuinely had our backs.

It was like a weight had been lifted. I had time to focus on the little things that made me happy. I started going out more, spending time with friends, and remembering what it felt like to laugh freely, to enjoy life without any worries. I wasn't just "the mom" anymore. I was a woman rediscovering herself—learning who she was outside of all the roles she had played for so long. And in that space, I felt like I was finally finding my true self again.

I also loved seeing how much my boys thrived in this new environment. They were happy, I was happy, and it felt like we were creating something amazing together. Life wasn't perfect, but it was ours. And that was enough.

The years seemed to pass in the blink of an eye. Before I knew it, I was 27, and for the first time in my life, I felt like I was truly living. My eldest had started school, my youngest was settled in nursery, and everything just felt… right. Life was no longer a constant uphill battle—I had built something stable, something happy. I had my own home, my boys were thriving, and I finally had the space to breathe.

I was enjoying my freedom in a way I never had before. For so long, my life had been consumed by relationships, responsibilities, and survival. But now, I had balance. I was still a devoted mother, but I also had a little time to be just me. The odd weekend out with friends felt like a luxury, a chance to let my hair down and enjoy the moments I had once missed out on. It was refreshing. And I was lucky to have the support of my dad and stepmom, who would happily take the boys for a night here and there, giving me that rare but much-needed time to myself.

I felt like I had grown into a whole new person—stronger, more confident, and in control of my own happiness. For the first time, I wasn't relying on anyone else. I was doing it all on my own, and I was proud of that.

But life, as always, had a way of throwing unexpected twists my way.

I still remember the exact moment I saw those two lines staring back at me on the pregnancy test. My stomach dropped.

I was on contraception—granted, a different kind this time since the first had clearly failed me—but apparently, birth control and I just weren't meant to get along. And no, this wasn't a reunion with the boys' dad—that ship had not only sailed, it had sunk to the bottom of the ocean. This pregnancy wasn't the result of love, or even a relationship. It was just one of those reckless, carefree nights, a moment of fun between two people with no attachments and no intentions of anything more.

And yet, here I was. Pregnant. Again.

I didn't know what to feel at first. Shock? Definitely. Fear? Maybe a little. But strangely, there was also a part of me that wasn't completely panicked. Unlike the first two times, I wasn't as young and I wasn't in a toxic relationship. I was independent, stable, and capable. And deep down, I knew I was going to be okay.

This wasn't part of my plan, but if life had taught me anything, it was that plans rarely worked out the way you expected them to.

When I told him I was pregnant, his response was immediate and absolute—he wanted nothing to do with the baby. No hesitation, no second thoughts. Just a cold, matter-of-fact statement that this wasn't something he wanted.

And honestly? That was fine by me.

I had already made up my mind. This baby was mine, and I was keeping them no matter what. I wasn't going to beg, convince, or try to change his mind. It was his choice, just like it was mine. If he wanted to walk away, that was on him. But I wasn't going to let his decision define how I felt about this pregnancy.

There was no argument, no back-and-forth, no drama. He made his choice, and I accepted it. No more needed to be said.

Because at the end of the day, I had already built a life for myself and my boys without needing a man to complete it. And if this baby was coming into the world with just me as their parent, then that was more than enough.

This pregnancy felt different. It was calm, peaceful—almost like a breath of fresh air. There was no stress, no drama, just me embracing every moment, enjoying the journey. My boys were over the moon, constantly talking about the baby growing in my belly, guessing whether they'd have a little brother or sister. Their excitement made it all the more special.

When New Year's Eve arrived, I decided to bring them along with me to find out the gender of our new addition. It felt like the perfect way to end one year and step into the next—with a moment that would change our lives forever.

As I lay there, watching the screen, my heart pounded in anticipation. And then, there it was—clear as day.

IT WAS A GIRL.

Omg. A perfect little girl.

I couldn't believe it. A daughter. My boys were getting a baby sister. I was going to have a little girl. A wave of happiness washed over me, and in that moment, everything felt complete.

After everything I had been through with my first two labours—the fear, the complications, the emergency C-sections—I knew I couldn't go through that again. This time, there would be no panic, no last-minute rush, no uncertainty. It was decided that I would have a planned C-section.

For the first time, I had a set date—a moment I could count down to, a day I knew for certain I would become a mom to my beautiful baby girl.

May 8th.

It felt surreal knowing exactly when she would arrive. There was no wondering, no waiting for contractions to start, no guessing when I'd need to drop everything and rush to the hospital. This time, I could prepare, I could plan, I could be ready.

And honestly? May 8th could not come quick enough.

The excitement grew every single day. My boys would talk to my belly, telling their little sister how much they couldn't wait to meet her. I found myself daydreaming about what she would look like, what her tiny cries would sound like, how it would feel to finally hold her in my arms.

For once, everything felt calm. No stress, no drama—just pure anticipation and happiness.

The day had finally arrived, the day I would meet my baby girl. Unlike my past labours, there was no panic, no rushing, just a quiet sense of anticipation as I prepared for the surgery. But what made the day even more special was having my sister by my side.

She was my rock that day, keeping me calm, making me laugh, and reminding me that everything was going to be okay. I couldn't have asked for a better person to be with me in that moment.

And then, she was here. My **perfect baby girl**.

As soon as she was born, my sister got to see her first, to witness her tiny fingers, her delicate features, her very first moments in this world. And in a moment, I'll never forget, she was also the first to feed her. Watching my sister care for my daughter with so much love and tenderness filled my heart in a way I can't even put into words.

She was incredible that day—strong, supportive, and completely selfless. I will always be grateful that she was the one standing beside me, sharing in the most precious moment of my life.

CHAPTER 9

After bringing my baby girl into the world, life felt so different—but in the best way possible. I was now a mother of three, balancing the chaos of school runs, sleepless nights, and endless cuddles. My boys were besotted with their little sister, always wanting to help, always protective of her. Watching them bond made my heart swell.

This time around, I was in such a different headspace. I had no relationship drama, no unnecessary stress—just me and my babies, building the life I had always wanted for us. I was proud of how far I had come, proud of how I was doing it on my own.

But despite everything, despite how much I had accomplished and how much I loved my children, there was this quiet longing inside me. A feeling that something was missing. I loved being a mom, but I also missed being me—the woman, the person who wasn't defined by motherhood alone. I started to feel like my entire existence revolved around my children, and while they were my everything, I also needed to find a little bit of myself again.

It was during this time that **Blackberry Messenger** became the backdrop to a new chapter in my life. It feels strange now, thinking about it, how quickly technology and social media can weave their way into our emotions. But back then, it was the easiest way to connect with someone outside of the world I had built. I started chatting with a guy on there, and from the start, he said all the right things—the things I hadn't heard in so long. He told me I deserved someone who wanted me just as much as I wanted them. He made me feel seen, heard, and for once, wanted.

Months passed, and we texted constantly, building up this connection. He made me feel special in a way that no one had in a long time, and it felt like this comforting escape from the pressures of being a single mom. In a way, he made me feel like I could have both worlds—that I could be the strong, independent mom, but also someone who could have a life outside of motherhood.

Eventually, we met up in person. The chemistry was immediate—everything just seemed to fall into place. We spent time together, talked for hours, and before I knew it, things were moving incredibly fast. The intensity of it all was overwhelming in the best way. He was charming, he made me laugh, and most importantly, he made me feel like I mattered.

Before I could even catch my breath, he was practically living with us. It felt exciting—like I had finally found someone who could fill the hole I hadn't even known was there. But deep down, there was this nagging feeling. I should've seen the signs. It was happening too quickly, too easily. A part of me knew it wasn't the way things were supposed to go, but I was so caught up in the whirlwind of attention and affection that I ignored it.

I was hungry for validation, for connection, for someone to make me feel more than just a mom. But I was blinded by the instant gratification of it all. I should've listened to my gut, to the feeling that something didn't add up. I rushed into something I wasn't ready for, all because I wanted to feel wanted in a way I hadn't in so long.

It wasn't about him, not really—it was about me not being okay with being alone. I didn't want to be alone in a world that I had fought so hard to build. And in that search for companionship, I ignored the fact that the timing wasn't right, that the intensity was a red flag. But in the moment, I was too eager to grab onto something that felt like it could make me feel whole again.

Things seemed okay at first. I had gotten caught up in the excitement of him being in my life, in the idea that things were finally falling into place. He fit in well with my children—they liked him, and he was kind to them. At first, everything appeared to be fine. I had hoped that this was the start of something good, that maybe this time things could be different. But, as always, the reality started to shift as the days passed.

When the day ended and it was just us at home, something else emerged. He would turn into a completely different person—controlling, paranoid, and demanding. The worst part was that I ignored it for a while, told myself it wasn't a big deal, that it was just him being protective. But it was much more than that. He needed to know everything I was doing—every moment of the day. If I was texting someone, he wanted to know who and what we were talking about. If I was on the phone, it was the same. There was no privacy, no space for me to just be me. It was suffocating.

It didn't stop there. If I went out to drop the boys off to school, he'd demand picture proof—every time. It didn't matter where I was or what I was doing; he had to see evidence of it. And when he went off to work, and it was just me and my daughter at home, that's when the pressure really hit. He would text me constantly, asking for pictures of me and my daughter just to prove we were home, doing exactly what I said we were doing. It was like his paranoia was invading every corner of our lives, suffocating everything in its path.

I knew, deep down, that this wasn't right. I knew he had to leave—it was eating me alive. There were nights I would sit up, trying to figure out how to get out without hurting my kids, without turning everything upside down. I packed his things up, put them outside while he was at work, hoping that once he saw it, he'd realize things had to end. But every time, it was the same routine. He'd call, he'd show up, and he would play the same card: "I moved here for you. I have nowhere else to go." The guilt would hit me hard. I didn't want to be cruel, didn't want to be the one who sent him away without a plan. But deep down, I knew I couldn't live this way anymore.

Each time he used that line, the guilt overwhelmed me, and I let him stay. But it was never the right choice. His behaviour was a constant reminder that no matter how much I wanted things to work out, they just weren't meant to. The fear of being alone again crept back in, but I had to remember—I was never truly alone. I had my kids, and that's all I needed.

The paranoia and control had continued to suffocate me, and that Christmas, a day that should have been filled with love and joy, ended up being a nightmare. Every year, we went to my dad and stepmom's house for dinner, a tradition I cherished. This year, he came along, playing the role of the perfect partner, but I couldn't shake the feeling that something was off. No one had seen his true colours yet, and I was hoping it would stay that way, but deep down, I knew better.

As the evening wore on, things started to change. I could hear the shift in the atmosphere—the tension in their voices. My dad, an older man in his early 70s, was trying to keep up with a man in his 20s. Both of them were drinking in the kitchen, and it quickly became clear that it wasn't going well. The laughter had turned to irritation, and soon enough, anger seeped into their words.

My stepmom and I tried to calm things down, but it was clear that wasn't going to work. And then, things escalated. There were shoves. It felt like the ground beneath me was shifting, and I knew, I just knew, that things were about to spiral out of control. We managed to get him out of their house, but I couldn't help feeling this heavy dread in my stomach. We called a taxi, and I left with the kids, heart pounding, terrified of what might be waiting for us when we got home.

My stepmom stayed on the phone with me, offering reassurance as I made my way back. She wanted to make sure we were safe. I tried to push aside the fear, but I couldn't ignore the constant anxiety building inside me. When we got home, everything seemed fine for a brief moment. I got the kids to bed, trying to keep everything calm, but then it happened.

I had just walked downstairs when I heard it. The banging. It was on my front door, harsh and unrelenting. My heart raced. I froze, paralyzed by fear. What was he going to do? My stepmom was still on the phone with me, trying to keep me calm, telling me everything would be okay, that I shouldn't open the door. But the banging didn't stop. It just grew louder, more frantic. I was terrified. The kids were asleep, and I didn't want anything to happen to them, but I also couldn't ignore what was happening at my front door.

I felt like I had no choice but to let him in. I hid my phone, but I kept the call with my stepmom open, hoping she could hear everything and would somehow help me. As soon as I opened the door, all hell broke loose.

The violence was so quick, so brutal. I was punched, kicked, and spat on, all in a matter of moments. I couldn't even process it. I just felt the pain and the shock. It was like I had become a stranger to myself. I was standing there, crying my eyes out, wondering what I had done to deserve this. What had I done wrong?

But he wasn't finished. After the physical assault, he moved into the living room, trashing everything in sight. Glass shattered. Furniture was destroyed. I just stood there, paralyzed, unsure of what to do. I was a broken shell, unable to do anything except cry. I could hear the crash of everything being torn apart, but all I could think about was my kids, asleep upstairs, unaware of the chaos that was unfolding below them.

And then, the front door swung open. It was my stepmom. She had heard the commotion and had gotten into a taxi to come to my aid. She walked in and saw the destruction, heard the chaos, and when he tried to deny everything, she told him, flat out, that she had heard it all. She knew what he had done, and she wasn't going to let him get away with it.

He didn't take kindly to that. The shame was too much for him to handle, so he left, but not before my stepmom stayed by my side. She helped me clean up the mess—the emotional and physical wreckage—before the kids woke up the next morning. I felt like I was floating, detached from the world, but I was trying to hold it together for them.

He was gone, for now, but in the back of my mind, I knew that I couldn't ever be sure for how long. The damage was done. I had to figure out how to move forward, but the question kept echoing in my mind: How could something so right, so perfect at the beginning, end up so wrong?

It wasn't long before he was back, just like I feared. He showed up with his apologies, his promises that he'd never do it again, and all the same hollow words. At that point, I felt numb to it all. I didn't want to believe him, but I was trapped in this cycle. I let him talk me around, convincing myself that maybe he really had changed. I forgave him. It seemed easier than facing the truth.

For the next couple of months, things seemed *normal*. Well, as normal as it could be. I had learned how to manage his paranoia, pretending like it didn't affect me. As long as I could keep the pain hidden, keep the kids from seeing how much he was controlling me, maybe everything would be okay. But deep down, I knew it wasn't.

Then came that night.

I was lying in bed when I heard him downstairs, his voice rising, full of rage. My daughter woke up crying, and instinctively, I went to her, holding her close. I don't know why I thought going downstairs would be a good idea, but I did. What I saw made my blood run cold. He was standing by the gas cooker, the knobs turned on but no flame. And he had a lighter in his hand.

"I know you're cheating on me. I'm going to kill you and your kids. If I can't have you, no one can," he screamed, his words slurred and wild.

I froze. I knew he was high, probably on something, but it didn't make his threats any less terrifying. I begged him to calm down, pleaded with him to stop, but it was like talking to a wall.

Before I knew it, his hands were around my throat, choking me, forcing me toward the stairs. And all I could do was hold my one-year-old daughter in my arms, terrified for both of us. I remember seeing my boys at the top of the stairs, their faces full of fear, and in that instant, I passed out.

I don't know how long I was unconscious, but when I came to, everything felt wrong. My daughter was screaming in my arms. I couldn't see my boys anymore, and panic flooded me. Where were they? I had to protect her. I had to get out of there.

I somehow got to my feet and, with my daughter still in my arms, ran out of the house. I screamed for help. I thought, maybe, someone would hear me. But no one did. My cries echoed in the empty street, and I realized I was completely alone, with him just behind me. I was so scared, terrified that he would finish what he started.

Then, in a moment of desperation, I remembered my phone. I had it in my pocket. My hands were shaking as I unlocked it and dialled 999, praying they'd hear me, even though I couldn't say a word. I just left the call on, praying it was enough.

I begged him to stop. I begged him to just let us go, but he wouldn't listen. And then, through the panic, I heard sirens. The police had arrived. My desperate call for help had been heard.

The rest of that night is a blur. I remember the chaos, the confusion, and the overwhelming relief when the police took control. But it wasn't until the next day that the full weight of what had happened hit me.

My youngest son came up to me, his face full of concern. He told me that, in the middle of everything, he had wanted to come and protect me. But his older brother had told him to go back to bed, to try and sleep. That broke my heart into pieces. My five-year-old son, just a little boy, felt the need to protect me in the middle of something he couldn't possibly understand.

It made me realize, in that moment, how much my children had already been affected by the things I had allowed into our lives. They shouldn't have had to carry that burden, yet here they were, trying to protect me when they should have been safe, asleep in their beds. The weight of that realization crushed me, and I promised myself I would never let them feel like that again.

CHAPTER 10

After everything I had been through with him—the manipulation, the control, the abuse—there was no way I was going back. Even though he begged me, I stood firm. I was done. He found a flat not too far from mine, and we kept in touch on a surface level. But for me, I was focused on moving forward. I started taking driving lessons, something I'd always wanted to do but never had the chance. It was exhilarating. I could feel the freedom inching closer. Soon, I'd be able to drive anywhere, go wherever I wanted. No more waiting for lifts, no more depending on anyone. I was doing it for me and my kids.

I also made a big decision: I wanted to be sterilized. I had three beautiful children, and I didn't want any more. My family was complete. I had no desire for more. I'd been through enough, and I was ready to take control of my future.

The decision to ask him for help, even with everything he'd put me through, is something I still don't fully understand. I guess, in that moment, I felt like he was the only one around. We had been on good terms for a little while, and it felt like the easy thing to do. I needed someone to watch the kids while I went into the hospital for the procedure, so I asked him.

But then, something unexpected happened. The girl from my first children's home, the one I used to fight with—she turned up to help. Over the years, we'd kept in touch, but we weren't super close. Still, she seemed like a safe bet. She drove, and she offered to pick me up from the hospital afterward. I was confused by the situation. When she arrived to pick me up, she was with him and my daughter. My heart sank. I'd left my daughter with my friend—so why was she here with them? They explained that they'd left the boys with a neighbour because they couldn't all fit in the car. I didn't know what to think, but at that point, I was exhausted, in pain from my procedure, and just wanted to get home.

Once we were back at my house, I thought everything would be okay. I'd get some rest, thank him for helping with the kids, and move on with my life. But things quickly escalated. He started ranting at me, calling me a "bitch" for getting the operation, claiming I had done it just to spite him because he wanted to have a baby with me. The words stung, but they didn't compare to what happened next. Without any warning, he slapped me across the face, then punched me right in my stomach, where my stitches were. The pain was unbearable. I couldn't believe this was happening again. I thought I had moved past this, thought I was finally free.

But something inside me snapped. I stood up, feeling weak and shaky, but there was a fire in me now. I wasn't going to let him hurt me again. I screamed at him to leave and pushed him as hard as I could. Somehow, I managed to summon the strength to get him out of my house. That was it. The door slammed behind him, and I knew, deep down, that I was never going to let him back into my life.

The next day, my friend, the one who had been watching my daughter, called me. She explained what had happened while I was at the hospital, and it made my stomach turn. She had FaceTime him so my daughter could talk to her brothers, and when he answered, my friend noticed something strange. He was in my bedroom—something she thought was odd since I hadn't been there. Then, as he moved the camera, she saw the girl from my first children's home lying on my bed. Why was she in my bedroom, with him? The realization hit me like a ton of bricks. Not only had he betrayed me once again, but he had also involved her in a way I wasn't prepared for.

I don't know what was worse—the physical violence or the emotional betrayal. But what I did know was this: I was done. He was gone, and there was no way in hell I was going to let him back into my life.

Getting over all the trauma he caused wasn't easy. It took so much time, so much effort, but I fought for my peace, for my freedom. I had been through hell, but I wasn't going to let it break me. I had come so far, and I wasn't about to let anything—or anyone—stand in my way.

At 30, I was finally driving. Maybe a little later than most, but I didn't care. The feeling of being behind the wheel, of taking control of my own life, was nothing short of exhilarating. For so long, I had been stuck—waiting for rides, relying on public transport to get by. But now, I could take my babies to school and nursery myself. No more relying on schedules, no more waiting for buses. I could go where I wanted, when I wanted. The world felt like it was opening up to me in a way it never had before.

My boys' dad had offered me a little run-around car until I could save up enough to get my own. I was beyond grateful. It wasn't much, but it was a symbol of my independence. Every time I got behind the wheel, I felt like I was closer to the life I had always dreamed of—one where I didn't have to look over my shoulder, where I wasn't stuck in a cycle of fear and dependence.

It wasn't perfect, but it was mine. And that felt like freedom.

The years that followed felt like a fresh start, and I couldn't help but marvel at how far I had come. For so long, I had been in survival mode, but now, for the first time, I could truly breathe. I was finally *me*—the me I had always wanted to be. The weight of my past was no longer dragging me down, and I could look forward to the future with hope and excitement.

One of the biggest changes was seeing all three of my babies in full-time school. It was bittersweet, yet overwhelmingly freeing. Watching them walk through those school gates every morning filled me with a mix of pride and disbelief. I had done it—somehow, despite everything I had been through, I had raised three healthy, happy children who were ready to take on the world. I didn't have to rush anymore, didn't have to juggle the chaos of being a stay-at-home mom and struggling to make ends meet. They were now in school, and it was their time to learn and grow, while I finally had time to focus on myself.

The moment I dropped them off at school, I felt a shift in my life. I was no longer just a mom; I was a woman with ambitions, with my own identity separate from motherhood. For the first time in years, I had space—both physically and emotionally—to think about what I wanted and where I wanted to go. It was a strange feeling, almost like freedom, but it also came with the responsibility of making the most of it. I had dreams, goals, and I wasn't about to let them slip away.

That's when I started working at the café. It wasn't just a job—it was an opportunity for me to reclaim a part of myself that had been lost for so long. My friend and her sister owned the café, and I was so grateful to be there. It wasn't easy, but it felt right. I wasn't just making money; I was building something for myself. The days I spent there gave me a sense of purpose I hadn't realized I needed. I was working alongside people I trusted, making my own income, and feeling valued for what I could contribute.

Balancing work with motherhood was challenging, but it felt like a step in the right direction. I wasn't just doing it all for my kids—I was doing it for myself. I felt like I was finally creating a life where I could give them the best of me, but also take care of myself, too. It was a delicate balance, but it was one I was figuring out every day.

And then there was the car. It wasn't just a vehicle—it was my newfound freedom. When I bought it, I realized how far I'd come. There was no more relying on public transport, no more waiting for rides. I had my own wheels, my own space, and it was all mine. I had worked hard to pay for it, and even though it was on finance, it was a symbol of everything I had fought for. It wasn't just the independence of having a car—it was the independence to live on my own terms, to take my kids wherever we needed to go without depending on anyone else.

I could finally take my kids to school, run errands, and go to work—all without feeling stuck or helpless. It was an exhilarating feeling, to know that I could handle it all on my own. Every small step, from dropping the kids off at school to clocking in at work, felt like a victory. I wasn't just surviving—I was thriving. I had built a life for myself and my children, and it was something I could be proud of.

Looking back, I could see how far I had come. I wasn't just a mom anymore—I was a woman who was working, growing, and creating the life she deserved. It wasn't always easy, but it was real. And for the first time in a long time, I knew I was exactly where I was meant to be.

CHAPTER 11

It was 2020, the year the world was shaken to its core by the onset of the COVID-19 pandemic. Life as we knew it came to a screeching halt. I was still working at the café, managing the daily grind, when the news broke that businesses and schools would be closing their doors indefinitely. It was a surreal moment, like something out of a dystopian movie, and I couldn't quite wrap my head around what was happening. Everything we had taken for granted—our routines, our normal ways of life—was suddenly upended.

Although the schools were shutting down, our café was categorized as a food establishment and allowed to stay open, but there was a catch. No customers could come inside. We could only offer takeout. It felt strange at first—serving food with no one sitting at the tables, no bustling atmosphere, just the hurried click of the kitchen and the hum of the coffee machine. It was still a job, but it was far from the environment I had known.

Juggling work and the kids being home from school was a struggle I hadn't anticipated. I had always been used to the routine of dropping them off, picking them up, and then having some space to focus on my own tasks. But now, with them home, it felt like everything was in constant motion. I was suddenly thrust into the role of both employee and teacher, trying to balance my responsibilities at the café with my newfound role as a homeschool mom. The constant interruptions, the fights over schoolwork, and the pressure of keeping them on track while I was trying to manage a job—it was overwhelming.

I couldn't turn to my dad or stepmom for help. They were isolating in their own bubble to stay safe, just like so many others. I understood, of course, but it didn't make it any easier. The fear of the virus was gripping everyone, and there was a sense of uncertainty that hung over all of us. I didn't want to put anyone at risk, especially not my family. It was scary for all of us, and I could feel the weight of that fear every day.

At times, I felt like I was drowning, pulled in a million directions, and yet trying to keep my head above water. My kids, who were used to school and their own structure, were just as lost as I was. I had to figure out how to keep them engaged, focused, and learning, all while worrying about my job, my health, and the well-being of my family. We were all in this together, yet it still felt incredibly isolating.

But even in the midst of all the chaos, I kept pushing forward. I had no choice. The world might have come to a standstill, but I still had to move. For my kids, for me, for the life I was building. Each day was a new challenge, but also a new opportunity to find strength in the face of uncertainty.

With all the chaos and uncertainty in the world, something unexpected happened—something that brought a bit of light into my life. It started with this guy who came into the café every day, without fail, for his regular cup of tea and a sandwich on his lunch break. He ran his own business, and, let's be honest, he was absolutely gorgeous. I couldn't help but notice him each time he came in, and though I'd always been friendly, I never thought much more of it. But little did I know, our paths were about to cross in a way that would change everything.

One day, after my shift, I ran into him outside. The sun was beaming down, blinding me just enough that I could barely see his face properly. I squinted at him, jokingly asking if I could borrow his Ray-Bans for a moment. He laughed, shaking his head, and replied, "Nah." But then, in a playful gesture, he said he had a spare pair in his van if I wanted to borrow them. I didn't hesitate, saying yes and following him to the van, curious to see these sunglasses.

When he handed them to me, I couldn't help but chuckle. They were ridiculous—bright, plastic sunglasses with ganja leaves plastered all over them. Not exactly my style, but I didn't care. I laughed and thanked him, joking about how they were more for a kid than an adult, but I wore them with pride anyway, feeling a bit silly but happy.

Later that day, I was at home, finally sitting down after the long day, when I got a message notification on Facebook. My heart skipped a beat when I saw it was from him. Oh my God, he had never messaged me before! I immediately messaged my friend who I worked with, feeling giddy with excitement. I told her what had just happened, and she responded with laughing emojis, telling me "I knew you fancied him."

His first message to me read, *"I hope you still have my sunglasses and are keeping them safe."* I couldn't help but laugh at the absurdity of it all, and I quickly replied, *"Oh, I'm so sorry, I lost them on my drive home, lol!"* It felt light and playful, and I couldn't believe I was actually having this kind of conversation with him.

Before I knew it, the conversation turned into something more. He asked if I wanted to meet up for a drink, and I couldn't believe my luck. My boys were with their dad, and my daughter was at a sleepover so I was free. It felt like the stars were aligning. I agreed, and he picked me up from my house.

We drove out to a countryside pub, where the world seemed to slow down around us. The drive was comfortable, easy. I was nervous but excited, unsure of what would happen, but trusting the flow of things. When we arrived, we spent hours talking and laughing, as if we had known each other for years. The conversation was effortless, and every moment felt natural, like it was meant to be. It was a beautiful feeling, one I hadn't experienced in a long time. The world outside was still in chaos, but for a few hours, it was just the two of us, enjoying the simplicity of a drink, a conversation, and the laughter that filled the air.

For the next couple of months, we went on a lot of dates. It felt so good to have someone who made me feel wanted again after all the years of being on my own. I was falling for him, and I couldn't help but feel both excited and a little bit nervous. At 34, with my past and my kids, I kept thinking, "Why would any man want to be with someone like me, with all my baggage?" But he never made me feel that way. In fact, he made me believe that I deserved the love I was receiving. Slowly, my self-doubt started to fade, and I began to believe that maybe, just maybe, I could have the life I always dreamed of. I was happy—genuinely happy—for the first time in a long while.

But then, in November of 2020, everything changed. It was just another afternoon. I was sitting in Costa Coffee with him and two of my friends, enjoying a warm drink and light conversation, when my phone rang. I looked at the caller ID and saw it was my stepmom. That was odd. She never called me; she only ever messaged. A sense of unease crept up as I answered the call, still trying to smile and keep the mood light. But when I heard her voice, I immediately knew something was wrong.

She told me that my dad was in the hospital. His breathing had gotten bad, and the doctors were doing everything they could to help him. But she wasn't sure what was going to happen. She told me he was fighting, but they weren't allowing anyone to visit him because of the restrictions—because of COVID-19. That hit me like a ton of bricks. I couldn't be there with him; I couldn't hold his hand or reassure him that everything would be okay. Nobody could. He was in the hospital, alone, isolated, while the world outside was in chaos. My heart felt like it was shattering.

When the call ended, I just sat there, frozen. My friends and my new now boyfriend were trying to console me, offering their words of comfort, telling me that the hospital staff would be taking good care of him. They said everything would be okay. But their words felt hollow. How could everything be okay when I couldn't be with my dad, when no one could be with him? The fear and helplessness hit me hard. I wasn't allowed to visit him; nobody was. The isolation we were all feeling because of the pandemic, it was now something that was keeping me from the most important person in my life. I didn't know what to do with all that emotion, that overwhelming sense of loss, when I couldn't even be there for him.

I just wanted to be with my dad, to make sure he knew I was there, to hold his hand and tell him everything would be okay. But instead, all I could do was wait, just like everyone else, feeling like I was losing control over the one thing that mattered most. The world felt like it was spinning out of control, and I couldn't stop it.

In October, I had made the heart-wrenching decision to quit my job. The chaos of the kids being constantly in and out of school due to COVID-19 was wearing me thin. It wasn't just the stress—it was the emotional toll of trying to keep it together for them when everything around us was falling apart. Every time one of them had to isolate, I had no choice but to stay home. It felt like I was failing them and myself, and no matter how hard I tried to juggle it all, I couldn't keep up. They were struggling too. I could see it in their eyes—the confusion, the fear, the sadness at being separated from their friends. And me? I was just trying to survive.

The days stretched on, endless and grey. Each morning, I'd wake up, trying to rally, trying to pretend like everything was normal, but inside, I was crumbling. The constant phone calls to the hospital for updates on my dad were draining. One minute, I'd hear that he was improving, and the next, it was like the ground would fall out from under me when I'd hear he wasn't doing well. It was the emotional whiplash I wasn't prepared for, and it felt like I was living in a constant state of limbo, never knowing what the next moment would bring.

But I held on. I clung to hope. I had to.

And then, on the evening of November 7th, something happened that I will never forget. I finally managed to get a FaceTime call with my dad. It was everything and nothing at the same time. Seeing him, still my dad, yet not the same man I had known, laying there in that hospital bed with all the tubes and the machines—his face pale and his eyes distant. He tried to smile, tried to make me feel like everything would be okay, even though I could see the exhaustion in his eyes. He asked about me and the kids, trying so hard to keep the conversation light, like it was just any other day. I told him we were fine, but I could feel the lump in my throat that I didn't dare speak aloud. I told him I loved him, and in that moment—maybe for the first time ever—he said it back. "I love you," he said. I can't even begin to describe what that moment did to me. It was everything I had ever needed to hear. He had never said those words before—not once in my life—and now, when I needed it the most, it felt like he was finally giving me something I'd always longed for.

"I love you," he said, and I couldn't help but break down.

The next morning, the phone call came. It was the hospital, and they told me what I had been dreading—my dad wasn't going to make it. They said I could come in to see him, but only two people could go. It would be me and my older stepsister. I barely processed the words; I just knew I had to get there, had to see him, even though I was terrified of what I might find.

I rushed to get ready, my hands trembling as I tried to pull myself together. My boyfriend, despite everything, was there for me. He drove me to the hospital, and even though I was falling apart inside, his presence was the only thing that kept me grounded. I couldn't imagine doing it without him. When we arrived, I was shaking, not just from the cold, but from the fear. We waited for my stepsister, and as soon as she arrived, we made our way to the front desk. We gave them my dad's name, and they handed us face masks, leading us into an empty waiting room. It felt like the air was thicker there, like time itself was slowing down, and I couldn't breathe. Why were we waiting? Where was my dad?

Then, a doctor came in. I couldn't see their face, only their eyes behind the mask. They spoke with such detachment, but I could feel the weight of their words before they even came. My stepsister and I braced ourselves, our hearts already knowing what was coming. And then, the words—words that shattered everything:

"We're so sorry, but your dad passed away 20 minutes ago."

NO. It couldn't be real. I didn't want to believe it. How could this happen? How could he be gone? I had just talked to him; just told him I loved him. I was supposed to see him again. I was supposed to have more time. But in that moment, the world around me disappeared. It was like a punch to the gut, and all I could feel was emptiness, a bottomless pit inside me.

My stepsister was frantic, begging for an apron and gloves so she could hold me. But I couldn't stand. My legs just gave way. I dropped to the floor, unable to do anything but feel the raw, gut-wrenching ache of it all. I couldn't stop crying, couldn't stop the pain. I could hear my stepsister's voice, trying to keep me calm, but I couldn't hear her. I couldn't hear anything except the deafening silence of my own grief. She held me, cradling me like a child, and for the first time in years, I let myself fall apart. I let the tears come, let the sobs tear through me, because there was no fighting it anymore.

It was over. My dad was gone.

And no matter how hard I tried to pull myself together, nothing could take away the fact that I'd never get to see him again, never get to hear his voice, never get to feel his presence in my life.

CHAPTER 11

Telling my children that their grandad had passed away was one of the hardest moments of my life. It felt like my heart shattered as I said those words. It was one thing to process my own grief, but to witness the pain of my kids made it all the more unbearable.

My daughter, only seven years old, had a deep, uncontrollable reaction. The moment I said it, her small face crumpled, and she burst into tears. Her sobs were heartbreaking, and as she clung to me, I could feel the weight of her loss, so pure and raw. My heart broke into a million pieces as I held her, trying to reassure her in the only way I knew how, but the truth was, I was just as lost as she was.

Then there were my boys, 11 and 13, trying their best to keep it together. I could see it in their eyes—the pain they were hiding. They tried to mask it, tried to be strong, but as their mom, I could see through their walls. They were broken, each of them processing the loss in their own way. It was as if the world around them had shattered, and there was no way to fix it. I wanted to take their pain away, to somehow make it easier for them, but I couldn't. All I could do was be there, to hold them when they let their guard down and show them that even though we had lost someone so important, we were still a family, and we would get through it together.

Through all of this, my boyfriend was there by my side. He was an absolute godsend during this time. He could see how hard I was struggling, but he never pushed me to talk or to feel differently. He just quietly supported me, and in many ways, he became the stability I so desperately needed. He was there for my kids, too helping them through their own grief in the way they needed it. I didn't know what I would've done without him. In the midst of my own devastation, he was the rock that kept me grounded, the shoulder I could lean on when everything else felt like it was crumbling.

As if losing my dad wasn't enough, the reality of the pandemic added another layer of heartbreak. We couldn't have a funeral. With the COVID-19 restrictions in place, we couldn't gather to grieve together or say our final goodbyes in the way we all needed. It felt so wrong. My dad deserved more than that, and so did our family. It felt like the grief was compounded by the isolation of it all. I couldn't hug my sisters the way I needed to, and I couldn't be with my stepmom to share the weight of the loss. Everything about it felt unnatural and so, so painful.

But as a family, we made a plan. My stepmom, my sisters, and I all agreed that come June 2021, on my dad's birthday, we would hold a small memorial in his honour. The restrictions were supposed to be lifted by then, and we would finally be able to gather, to be with one another, to grieve properly and to celebrate my dad's life. It wasn't the funeral we had hoped for, but it would be our way of coming together as a family, to comfort one another and say goodbye in the only way we could.

Even though we were all carrying the weight of our grief, I felt a sense of peace knowing that we had a plan to honour my dad's memory. I was grateful to my stepmom and sisters for their support during that time. We may not have been able to have the kind of closure we all longed for, but we were determined to make the most of the situation, to find some semblance of comfort in the small things, and to make sure that my dad knew, in his own way, that he was deeply loved, missed, and remembered.

Throughout all of this, my children kept me going. Their need for me, their dependence on me, forced me to keep putting one foot in front of the other. I couldn't let my grief consume me entirely because they needed me. I had to be there for them, just as they were there for me, even if we didn't always have the words to explain what we were all going through.

The pain of losing my dad never really left, but in time, the memories of him became something I could hold onto more gently. A piece of him would always be with me, woven into the love I had for my children. I saw him in their laughter, in the way they smiled, in the little moments that made life beautiful. He was there in the way my daughter's eyes lit up when she was happy, in the way my boys carried themselves with quiet strength. He would forever be a part of them, of us. Though he was gone, his presence would never fade—he lived on in them, in me, in the love we shared as a family.

As the months passed, I felt like a shadow of myself. The grief of losing my dad had settled deep into my bones, weighing me down in a way I had never experienced before. I wasn't me anymore. I withdrew from everything and everyone. I ignored calls from friends, stopped making plans, and barely spoke to anyone outside my home. The only people I could bring myself to care about were my kids and my boyfriend—they were the only ones keeping me going. But even with them, I felt like I was just going through the motions, barely present, barely holding on.

I knew I couldn't carry on like this. I didn't want my children to see me this way, lost in my own grief, unable to be the mother they needed. So, I finally did something I had been avoiding I booked a doctor's appointment. Due to the lingering COVID-19 restrictions, in-person visits were still limited, and only urgent cases were being seen face-to-face. I settled for a phone consultation and was scheduled with a doctor I had never spoken to before.

When she called, the warmth in her voice instantly put me at ease. For the first time in what felt like forever, I didn't feel so alone in what I was going through. As I spoke, pouring out the feelings I had been burying, she listened—really listened. I told her about my dad, about how I had shut myself off from the world, about how I was struggling to be the person I used to be. She gently asked if I had considered medication to help with my mood. In the past, I had always resisted the idea, convinced I could push through on my own. But this was different. I wasn't coping, and for the sake of my children, for the sake of myself, I knew I needed to try something.

By the end of the call, I felt something I hadn't felt in months—a small flicker of hope. The doctor arranged for me to start antidepressants and scheduled regular follow-up calls every two weeks to check on me. I wasn't magically better, but for the first time in a long time, I felt like maybe, just maybe, I could find my way back to myself again.

But healing wasn't instant. The first antidepressants didn't sit well with me. Some made me feel like a ghost in my own body, others kept me on edge, unable to settle. It was a slow and frustrating process of trial and error, and there were days I wanted to give up. But then, finally, I found the right one. It didn't take away my grief, but it softened the edges. It allowed me to get out of bed without feeling like I was carrying the weight of the world on my shoulders.

Slowly, I started living again. Not in the way I had before, but in small, significant ways. I could go to the shops without feeling overwhelmed. I could plan little day trips with my kids and my boyfriend without feeling like I was pretending to be okay. I could laugh, and this time, I didn't feel guilty for it. I wasn't completely myself again, but I was finding pieces of her. And through all of this, he was there. My beautiful, patient, understanding man. He never made me feel like I was too much. He stood by me through every breakdown, every tear-filled night, every moment where I thought I'd never be okay again.

And then, something incredible happened. As time passed, I watched him step into the role of a father for my little girl. It wasn't forced; it wasn't something I had asked of him—it was just natural. He adored her, and she adored him. They had their own special days together, just the two of them, building a bond that made my heart ache in the best way.

Meanwhile, my boys were spending more time at their dad's house. It was like something had shifted in him—like he had suddenly decided to step up and be the father they needed. And for the first time in a long time, everything seemed okay with the world.

Life wasn't perfect. It would never be the same. But for the first time since losing my dad, it felt okay. I still carried my grief, and I always would, but it no longer consumed me. I could breathe again. And for that, I was thankful.

CHAPTER 12

It had been just under eighteen months since my dad passed, and though the hurt still lingered, I had learned to carry it. Grief wasn't something that disappeared—it was something that settled into you, becoming part of who you were. Some days, it felt like a dull ache in the background, and other days, it hit like a fresh wound. But I was managing. I was surviving.

The antidepressants had helped in some ways, but there was one thing I hadn't been prepared for—the weight gain. At first, I tried to ignore it, telling myself it wasn't a big deal, but every time I looked in the mirror, I felt worse. It was as if I had swapped one struggle for another. My body didn't feel like mine anymore, and instead of lifting me out of depression, the weight gain was pulling me back down. I knew I needed a change.

Switching to a new medication wasn't easy. I was scared to start all over again, afraid of the side effects, afraid I'd feel worse before I felt better. But this time, I got lucky. The new medication helped in all the right ways—I still felt stable, my emotions weren't as overwhelming, and most importantly, the weight gain stopped. Losing the weight was another battle entirely, but instead of letting it break me, I let it fuel me. If I couldn't lose it easily, then I'd fight for it. I was more determined than ever to push myself, to get up, to go out, to take back control of my body and my mind.

As life slowly returned to normal after the chaos of COVID-19, it felt like the world was finally settling again. My kids were happy—that was the most important thing. Both my boys were in secondary school now, growing into young men before my eyes, and my little girl was still thriving in primary school, her bright energy lighting up every room she walked into. Seeing them happy, watching them grow, made every struggle worth it.

And then there was my man. Through everything, he had stayed by my side, steady and unwavering. Our love hadn't just survived the storm of my grief—it had grown stronger. And now, we had taken another step forward—he had moved in. Our home finally felt complete, like all the missing pieces had fallen into place.

For the first time in a long time, my life felt stable. I still carried my grief, but it no longer weighed me down. I had love. I had my children. I had this man who had become so much more than I ever thought possible. My little family was whole, and in a world that had once felt so broken, that was everything.

As life slowly began to feel good again, I knew deep down that I was finally moving in the right direction. There was a quiet contentment in my days, a feeling I hadn't experienced in years. I was finding my rhythm—being a partner, a mother, and navigating my grief in a way that no longer swallowed me whole. I felt stable. At peace.

Then, out of nowhere, a message arrived that shattered that peace in an instant.

It was from someone I never thought I'd hear from—my mom's eldest son, my brother. My stomach tightened as I read his words, each one hitting me like a gut punch.

"Mum's dying. You should come see her."

I froze. For a moment, I just stared at the message, my heart pounding in my chest. My mind couldn't make sense of it. It didn't feel real. My mom? Dying? It felt like a cruel trick, like the universe was playing some sick joke. This was the woman who had caused me so much pain, who had been a stranger to me for so many years. She had been a ghost in my life for so long, a shadow from my past that I had long since buried. And now, suddenly, she was disappearing for good.

My hands trembled as I reached for my phone. I needed answers. I needed to hear it from someone who could tell me this wasn't real. That this wasn't happening.

With shaky hands, I called the hospice in Taunton and when they picked up, I could barely get the words out. My voice cracked; my throat tight with something I couldn't quite name—was it grief? Fear? Or just the weight of a lifetime of unresolved pain crashing down on me all at once?

The nurse on the other end spoke softly, her voice laced with the kind of careful kindness that only confirmed what I already knew deep down. When the nurse gently confirmed it, my heart dropped. It was true. My mother had bowel cancer. She was in her final days. And there was nothing - nothing that could save her now.

I pressed a hand to my chest, as if that would stop the ache that was quickly spreading through me. I wasn't sure what I was supposed to feel. Was I supposed to cry? Was I supposed to grieve for the mother who had hurt me? The mother who had abandoned me?

Or was I supposed to let go of the past and be there for her now, when it was too late to fix anything?

The drive to Taunton felt like a lifetime. 133 miles, two and a half hours of silence, apart from the hum of the engine and the occasional squeeze of my partner's hand on mine. He knew I was lost in my own head. I barely blinked, barely breathed. My mind raced, but I couldn't hold onto a single thought for long enough to make sense of it.

What was I supposed to feel?

Anger for the years of pain? Sadness for the mother I never really had? Regret for not reaching out sooner?

I didn't know.

When we arrived at the hospice, a suffocating stillness settled over me. The air was thick, heavy, like it carried the weight of unspoken goodbyes. I forced my feet forward, step by step, heart pounding in my chest, until I reached her room. And then, I saw her.

I wasn't prepared.

She was unrecognizable.

The woman lying in that bed wasn't the mother from my childhood. She was frail, her once strong presence now reduced to fragile bones and hollow cheeks. Her skin looked paper-thin, almost translucent, stretched over a body that had already begun surrendering to death. She looked so small.

Memories hit me like a freight train. The past I had spent so long trying to bury clawed its way to the surface.

Not warm, comforting memories—no, those didn't exist. Instead, I saw flashes of a mother who came and went like a passing storm, unpredictable and destructive.   yet there were moments, rare and fleeting, where she was just *Mom*. A half-smile as she brushed my hair, the distant memory of her laughter filling a room, her holding her first grandson. But they were drowned out by everything else. By the neglect, by the pain, by the years of learning to survive without her.

And now, here she was. Dying.

A lump formed in my throat, my body frozen between the past and the present. I wasn't sure if I wanted to run to her or run away.

How do you grieve for someone who was never really there?

I stood at the doorway, my chest tightening, my breath shallow. This was my mother. The woman who gave birth to me, who shaped me in ways I wished she hadn't. The woman who had missed every milestone, every struggle, every tear I had cried without her.

And now, she was slipping away, and I had no idea what to do.

The first words out of her mouth were, *"Have you got a fag? I need a fag."*

I almost laughed through the lump in my throat. Here she was, lying frail and weak in a hospice bed, her body barely more than skin and bone, and all she could think about was a cigarette. It was so *her*. Even in this moment, when everything felt surreal, she was still the same in some way. It was a strange comfort—familiar in a sea of unfamiliar emotions.

But then reality hit again.

I looked at her properly, taking in the sight of the woman who had given me life, yet had been absent for so much of it. Her face, thinner than I'd ever seen, was marked with years I hadn't been there to witness. Memories I had buried deep began to surface, but there weren't many. The times she had drifted in and out of my life, the birthdays she had missed, the moments where I had needed a mother, and she simply wasn't there. And, despite it all, I was *here*.

I swallowed hard and forced myself to push through the storm raging inside me. *"Mum, this is my partner."*

The words felt heavier than I expected, like they carried the weight of all the things I had lost. I had never gotten the chance to introduce my dad to him. That thought burned in my chest. My dad would have *loved* him, I knew he would. He would have been so proud that I had finally found someone who treated me the way I deserved, who stood by me through everything. But he was gone. I would never get to see the approval in his eyes, never get to hear his voice telling me, *you've done good, love.*

And yet, here I was, introducing my partner to *her*.

She studied him for a moment, a small smile tugging at her lips despite her exhaustion. A flicker of something crossed her face—not quite sadness, not quite joy. Just something in between. She said that he looked like someone from my past, with a teasing glint in her tired eyes. She smiled at her own joke, and for a moment, it felt normal. We all smiled with her. her voice weaker than I remembered but still carrying that familiar teasing tone.

She smiled, and for a fleeting second, it felt like nothing had changed. Like we were just a mother and daughter having a simple conversation, sharing a moment. My partner squeezed my hand gently, grounding me, reminding me that I wasn't alone in this.

It wasn't how I had imagined introducing my mother to the man I loved. But then again, nothing about my relationship with her had ever been normal. And as much as it hurt, as much as it twisted something deep inside me, I held onto that moment, knowing it was all I was going to get.

That evening, we sat by her bedside and talked for hours. It felt strange—almost unnatural—how easily the conversation flowed despite the weight of the moment. She told me she had made me her next of kin, the executor of her will. The words hit me harder than I expected.

It was like a sudden jolt of reality. This wasn't just a visit. This wasn't just catching up after years apart. This was *goodbye*.

She was preparing for the inevitable, making sure things were in place for when she was gone. I nodded, trying to keep my expression neutral, but inside, it *hurt*. After everything, after years of distance and missed moments, it had come down to this—to me being the one to take care of things when she no longer could. I wasn't sure how to feel about it. Honoured? Angry? Heartbroken? Maybe all of them at once.

As the night wore on, exhaustion crept in, and my partner and I left to get some rest. It had been an emotional, draining day—one of the longest of my life.

The next morning, we were up early, ready to go back to the hospice. When we arrived, we were met at the entrance by a group of nurses and the hospice manager. Their kindness caught me off guard. They explained that instead of wasting money on hotels and B&Bs, we could stay in an unused apartment on the premises. The relief that washed over me was overwhelming. We had no idea how long we'd be here, and now, at least, we had somewhere to be close to her without added stress.

Seeing my mom again that morning felt different. A little less awkward, a little more real. But she was speaking less now. Her words were coming slower, her voice weaker. It was like watching time slip through my fingers, and there was nothing I could do to stop it.

Then, to my surprise, her ex husband—my stepdad—walked in.

I could see the shock flicker across her face, but beneath it, there was something else. Gratitude. A quiet happiness that, even in her final days, she was surrounded by people who had once been part of her life. He stayed with us for hours, sitting by her side, reminiscing, just *being* there. And not just that day—he came back, every day, while I was there. It meant something, to both of us.

And then, just when I thought I was holding it together, my best friend arrived.

She had been living in Devon, hours away, but somehow, she just *knew*. She always did. No matter what, no matter how much time had passed or where life had taken us, she had this way of showing up exactly when I needed her most.

As I hugged her, I felt the weight of everything press down on me, but I wasn't alone in carrying it.

Despite the sadness, the confusion, the mess of emotions I still hadn't figured out, I realized something—I wasn't facing this alone. I had my partner, my stepdad, my best friend. I had love and support around me, holding me up through the hardest goodbye.

Me and my partner had to get back. We had been there for three days, and as much as I wanted to stay by her side, life was still moving outside of this little bubble I had found myself in. The kids needed sorting, school runs had to be made, and normality—whatever that even was—had to be maintained. But I knew I wasn't done. I knew I needed to go back.

When we got home, we made a plan. My partner would stay with the kids, keep everything running smoothly, and I would return to Taunton. This time, I was going with my younger brother.

The brother I had only met a few years prior. The brother who had been adopted at birth, who had found me on Facebook, and who I had built this beautiful, unexpected bond with. We had never shared a childhood, never made those growing-up memories together, but somehow, we just *clicked*. He was my brother in every way that mattered. And now, here we were, about to face something so deeply personal—something that neither of us really knew how to navigate.

For him, it was even more complicated. He had never met our mother. He had never met his biological father. This wasn't just saying goodbye—this was hello and goodbye all at once.

He drove the long journey while I sat beside him, my mind tangled in thoughts I couldn't quite untangle. (I'd always hated motorway driving, so I was secretly grateful he had taken the wheel.) When we arrived, I was relieved to see we still had the apartment to stay in. A small comfort in a situation that offered so few.

But my brother wasn't ready.

He didn't go to see her straight away. I understood. How could you? How do you prepare yourself to walk into a room and meet the person who gave you life—only to say farewell in the same breath?

That first night, I sat with her alone. I went back and forth between her room and the apartment, checking in on my brother, waiting to see if he was ready. My mom was barely awake by then. When she did try to speak, her words were lost in slurred murmurs, like echoes of thoughts that never fully formed. I held her hand, watching her, knowing she was slipping further away, and still, it didn't feel real.

The next day, my brother finally went in.

I left him to it. This wasn't my moment—this was his.

We stayed for a few more days, taking turns sitting with her. Even my stepdad was back again, proving that no matter what had happened in the past, she wasn't going to leave this world alone. There was always someone there.

I felt like I had stepped into an entirely different reality, like I was living in some strange, suspended time where nothing else existed beyond these four walls, beyond the quiet beeping of machines and the soft whispers of nurses. I was literally *waiting* for my mother to die. And yet, she kept holding on. Clinging to something none of us could see.

On the last day, the day I planned to go home, I sat with her.

I held her hand and whispered to her, "It's okay, Mom. I'm ready to say goodbye. I'll handle this. You don't have to worry anymore."

I don't know if she heard me. I don't know if she understood. But I wanted her to know that whatever she was holding on for, she didn't have to anymore.

Me and my brother drove home. I was exhausted. Numb. When I finally got into bed that night, my body barely sank into the sheets before my phone rang.

I *knew* what this call was.

My stomach twisted violently, and for a moment, I hesitated. Even expecting it didn't make it any easier. I answered, and on the other end was the same lovely nurse I had said goodbye to only hours earlier.

She spoke gently, her voice soft, kind.

"Your mother has passed."

She told me it was peaceful. That she had been there with her in those final moments. That she wasn't alone.

I could feel my eyes filling with tears, but they wouldn't fall.

What was this feeling?

Had she *waited* for us to be home? Had she wanted to go when she knew we were all safe, when she knew we had left, when she knew we wouldn't see her take her last breath?

I didn't know how to feel.

Was I sad that I wasn't there? That I hadn't been by her side at the very end? Or was I relieved that I hadn't had to witness it?

I lay there, staring at the ceiling, the weight of it all pressing down on me.

She was gone.

CHAPTER 13

Going back to Taunton so soon after my mom's passing felt surreal. The grief hadn't even settled properly, yet here I was, being called back—not to mourn, but to clear out her house. The local council needed it emptied, and suddenly, I was responsible for dismantling the last physical traces of her life.

We arranged for the boys to stay with their dad and my daughter with my stepmom, and then my partner and I set off on that long drive again. The same road I had taken just days ago to say goodbye now carried me back to erase what was left of her. It felt cold, harsh—like she was being wiped away too quickly.

When we arrived, we decided to stay the night in the house. It was strange, stepping inside. It still smelled like her—her perfume, her cigarettes, her life. Her things were everywhere, untouched, as if she'd just stepped out for a moment and would be back soon. But she wouldn't be.

Sorting through her belongings was exhausting in every way possible. Every drawer opened, every cupboard emptied, felt like peeling away layers of history I had barely been part of. Old photos, clothes, trinkets—things she had once loved, things that had meant something to her, yet so little to me. What do you do when you're left with the remnants of someone you never truly knew?

Her neighbours were only just finding out she had passed. One by one, they came over, offering condolences, sharing small stories about her, painting a picture of a woman I barely recognized—one who was funny, who had friends, who was well-liked. It was odd hearing these things, knowing that side of her had existed for others but never for me.

Since we couldn't take her furniture back and had no use for it, we posted an ad on Facebook, offering it to anyone who needed it. Watching strangers come and take pieces of her life away felt strangely fitting—she had been in and out of mine so much, and now, even her belongings were slipping away just as easily.

As we drove around town dropping her clothes off at charity shops, we passed a pub called *The Black Horse.* A neighbour had mentioned it was her usual spot, saying if I had the chance, I should go in. So, I did.

The moment I spoke, the barmaid recognized me. She smiled, tilting her head as if seeing a ghost. "You sound just like her," she said. A pang of something deep and unfamiliar hit me in the chest.

Then the manager came down, and as soon as he saw me, he shook his head with a knowing smile. "You look just like your mom," he said. I didn't know how to respond. I had spent so long detaching myself from her, yet here I was, hearing how much of her was still in me.

He led me to a wall where they had just put up a plaque—a tribute to my mom. Next to it was a framed photo of her, laughing, a drink in hand, surrounded by people who clearly adored her. My throat tightened as I stared at it.

They told me a few stories about her—how she always had a joke, how she could light up a room, how she was a part of their little pub family. I smiled, nodded, but inside, my heart ached. I had spent so many years resenting her, keeping her at a distance, and yet here were all these people who had shared moments with her that I never got to.

It made me feel something I hadn't expected guilt.

Had I been too harsh? Had I wasted too much time? Could we have ever had a different ending?

I would never know.

As I left the pub, I carried those thoughts with me, heavier than anything I had packed up from her house.

A couple of weeks after clearing out my mom's house, we had to take another trip—this time to Weston-Super-Mare—to collect her ashes. I hadn't been able to pick them up from the funeral home in time since I lived too far away, so another family member had done it for me. Now, it was time to bring her home.

This time, we decided to take the kids. It was a beautiful day—the sun was shining, the sky was clear, and for a moment, it almost felt like just another family day out. My kids had only met my mom a handful of times, barely remembered her, and honestly, she had never played a big role in their lives. But if I was going to bring them along on this trip, I wanted to make sure they had a good day. I didn't want this to just be about grief.

When we arrived to collect her ashes, I felt this strange, heavy stillness settle over me. As they placed the urn in my hands, a wave of emotion hit me like a punch to the stomach. It was surreal—this was my mom, reduced to something so small, something I could hold. A person who had once been so full of life, even in her chaos, was now just ashes in my hands. I wasn't sure what to feel. Sadness? Anger? Regret? Maybe all of it at once.

I held onto them tightly, unsure if I was ready to let go, to fully accept that this was it. That she was gone. A part of me still didn't know how to grieve her properly. I had spent so much of my life without her, learning not to need her, that now, in death, she suddenly felt so present.

After collecting the ashes, we headed straight for the beach. The boys ran ahead, kicking a ball between them, while my daughter plopped herself down in the sand, determined to bury herself completely. For a little while, I just stood there, watching them, the urn still tucked away safely in my bag. It was such a contrast—this weight in my heart, the finality of holding my mom's remains, against the laughter of my children, the sun warming my skin, the sound of waves crashing softly in the distance.

And then my daughter spotted the donkeys. Her face lit up instantly, and she tugged on my arm, begging for a ride. I couldn't help but laugh—she was so excited, so full of life. It was exactly what I needed in that moment, a reminder that life keeps moving forward, even in grief.

After the beach, we grabbed some food and spent hours in the arcades. Watching the kids so happy, hearing their laughter, seeing them completely lost in the moment—it made me happy, too. It reminded me that, despite everything, despite the complicated relationship I had with my mom, I had built something beautiful for myself. A life full of love, of joy, of moments like this. And maybe that was enough. Maybe that was my closure.

Days passed, and the weight of grief settled in like a storm I couldn't outrun. I was only 36 years old, and now, both of my parents were gone. It wasn't just the loss of one or the other it was the finality of having no parents at all. My dad had only passed 18 months before, and now, here I was, struggling to process that I would never see either of them again.

I missed my dad so much. Some nights, I'd sit and scroll through old videos of the kids, just to hear his voice in the background. That warm, familiar Irish tone—it always made me feel safe, like no matter what, he was there. Now, all I had were these snippets, these tiny fragments of time where he still existed, where I could close my eyes and pretend, even for just a moment, that he wasn't really gone.

But grief is cruel, and it doesn't let you linger in just one place for too long. As soon as I started missing my dad, my mom's memory pushed its way in, like an unwelcome guest in my mind. The regret hit me hard—I would never get another chance to fix things, to repair what was broken between us. That door had been closed forever, and there was nothing I could do about it. My head felt like a mess, trapped in a cycle of missing, regretting, wishing things had been different.

And yet, through all the sadness, there was one thing that made me laugh. Sitting on my side table, right next to each other, were their urns—almost identical. The sight of them together like that made me giggle because I knew, without a doubt, they would have absolutely *hated* this. The thought of them bickering in the afterlife over being placed side by side was enough to bring a smile to my face.

Even in death, they found a way to make me laugh.

After my dad passed, I knew I needed to do something to keep a part of him with me forever. A tattoo felt like the right choice, even though he would have absolutely hated it—he hated that I had any at all. I could almost hear his voice in my head, grumbling about it, and that thought made me smile. But this wasn't just any tattoo; it was him.

When he was in the funeral home, I had them take his fingerprint. It was such a small thing, yet it meant everything. My tattooist carefully traced every ridge and curve, placing it perfectly within a heart on my forearm. The moment the needle touched my skin; I felt a strange mix of pain and peace. It was like he was with me again, like a part of him would always be right there. Every time I look at it, I feel that connection. It's more than just ink—it's him, imprinted on me forever.

So, when my mom passed, I knew I had to do the same. I wanted something that was hers, something that represented her in the way my dad's fingerprint did for him. She had always been obsessed with butterflies—delicate, beautiful, free. It just made sense. I decided on a simple butterfly within a heart, nothing elaborate, the same size as my dad's. One my arm, side by side, just like their urns sitting next to each other at home—though I know they both would have absolutely hated that too.

Tattoos have always been more than just art to me; they're how I tell my story, how I mark the things that matter. They're how I carry the pieces of my past that I refuse to let go of. Having both of them with me in this way brings me a comfort I can't quite put into words.

Sometimes, when the grief is too much—when I feel the weight of their absence pressing down on me—I run my fingers over the ink, tracing the lines, feeling their presence in a way I can't anywhere else. And in those quiet moments, I remember.

Losing both of my parents in such a short space of time left a hole in me that I didn't know how to fill. Grief is a strange thing—it creeps up on you when you least expect it, dragging you under when you think you're finally keeping your head above water. I was terrified of sinking into that darkness, of letting my past and my pain consume me.

That's when I found an escape in the most unexpected place—TikTok. At first, it was just a distraction, a way to pass the time, but before I knew it, it became something so much bigger. I started going live, meeting people from all over the country, laughing in ways I hadn't in so long. It was like stepping into a different reality, one where I wasn't the girl with a painful past or the woman carrying the weight of loss. I was just me, and that was enough.

TikTok gave me more than just a way to pass the time—it gave me connection. One person, in particular, stood out. She was funny, real, and we just clicked instantly. What started as casual chats in each other's lives quickly became something deeper. Before I knew it, we were talking every single day, not just on TikTok but on the phone for hours, sharing everything—our struggles, our jokes, our lives. It didn't matter that we had never met in person; I knew I had found a real friend. The kind that just gets you.

We talked constantly about meeting up, but life always seemed to get in the way. Then, my partner mentioned wanting to go camping. He had grown up camping as a kid and was determined for my daughter to experience it too. As soon as he brought it up, an idea sparked I knew exactly where we should go. My TikTok friend lived down south, and it was the perfect excuse to finally make our long-awaited meet-up happen.

The excitement was unreal. It wasn't just about finally meeting her; it was about everything this trip symbolized. A break from reality, a chance to experience something new, and a reminder that life still had beautiful moments to offer. I had been through so much, but this? This was something to look forward to. And after everything, I deserved that.

 The day had finally arrived, and we were all up bright and early, buzzing with excitement. I could barely sit still—my stomach was a mess of butterflies. This trip wasn't just about camping; it was about finally meeting someone who had become such a huge part of my life, even though we had never met in person. And to top it off, I was with two of my favourite people—my partner and my daughter.

I won't lie; I wasn't exactly thrilled about the whole camping idea. The thought of sleeping in a tent, battling the unpredictable British weather, and sacrificing my home comforts didn't exactly fill me with joy. But I knew this trip wasn't just about me—it was about giving my daughter an experience she'd never had. Watching her excitement made it all worth it.

When we finally arrived at the campsite, I was taken aback. It was like something straight out of a storybook—lush greenery stretched out before us, nestled perfectly between two woodlands. The air was fresh, the atmosphere calm, and for a moment, I just stood there, taking it all in. Maybe, just maybe, this wouldn't be so bad after all.

Pitching the tent, however, was a whole different story. As soon as we parked up and started unpacking, the bickering began. My partner and I went back and forth, each convinced we knew the best way to set up. He swore he had it under control, and I, of course, begged to differ. There were plenty of sighs, eye rolls, and maybe a few not-so-subtle digs thrown in, but we somehow managed to get the tent up without physically harming each other. That, in itself, was an achievement.

But despite all of it, my mind was elsewhere. As much as I was soaking in the beauty of the place, as much as I was trying to embrace the experience, there was only one thing I truly cared about in that moment—finally meeting my friend.

We knocked on the front door, and the second she opened it, all the nerves and anticipation melted away. There was no awkwardness, no hesitation—just warmth. We hugged like we had done it a dozen times before, like this wasn't the first time we were meeting in person but just another reunion between old friends. It felt so normal, so right, as if we had known each other in another lifetime.

Stepping inside, we were welcomed with open arms. She introduced us to her kids, and almost instantly, my daughter clicked with her eldest daughter. Watching them together, laughing and playing like they'd been friends forever, made my heart swell. There's something special about seeing your child form a bond so naturally—it made everything feel even more perfect.

We spent the afternoon in her garden, soaking up the sun, drinks in hand, chatting for hours like no time had passed at all. There was no pressure, no need to force conversation—it just flowed. We talked about everything, from our lives to our plans for the rest of the week. The weather was shaping up to be amazing, and we couldn't have picked a better time to be here. It truly felt like fate had aligned everything perfectly for this trip.

The next day, she and her kids came to the campsite, and we had everything ready—a barbecue, plenty of food, and a whole day of fun ahead. The kids ran wild in the massive open field, their laughter echoing through the air as they played without a care in the world. We, as adults, even found ourselves joining in, getting caught up in their games, reliving childhood for just a little while. It was one of those moments where you forget everything else—grief, stress, worries—and just exist in pure joy.

And then came *the* moment. I decided to take a break, plopped myself onto a camping chair... and went straight through it. One second, I was sitting down, and the next, I was on the ground, still clutching my drink, not spilling a single drop. The whole campsite erupted in laughter, but none louder than my friend, who was doubled over, holding her belly, absolutely howling. Phones were out, all eyes were on me, but instead of embarrassment, all I felt was pride—because my drink had survived the fall! *Priorities, right?*

That moment summed up everything about this trip—pure, unfiltered happiness.

The rest of the week was an adventure—exploring different beaches, feeling the sand between our toes, the salty breeze in our hair. We laughed our way through the funfair, the kids' excitement contagious as they ran from ride to ride. Shopping trips turned into little treasure hunts, finding bits and pieces to remember the trip by. Every single moment was filled with joy, surrounded by incredible people, and blessed with the most perfect weather. It was the kind of week that makes you forget about everything else—the kind that stays with you forever.

CHAPTER 14

Looking back on everything I've been through—the struggles, the heartbreak, the moments I thought I wouldn't make it—I realize just how far I've come. Life isn't perfect, but it's good. It's real. And most importantly, it's mine.

My partner and I have been together for almost five years now. We've had our ups and downs like any couple, but we've built something solid—something that feels like home. And my kids… my beautiful, incredible kids. They are my greatest achievement.

My eldest son, nearly 18 now, is growing into such a handsome young man. It's hard to believe that soon he'll be an adult himself. I see so much of myself in him, but also so much strength, kindness, and potential. My younger son, now 15, has grown into his own. School wasn't always easy for him—he had his moments of getting into trouble, being late, and pushing boundaries—but he's come such a long way, and I'm so proud of the person he's becoming. And then there's my daughter—almost 12, in full pre-teen mode. She's into makeup, hair, and spends hours on the phone with her friends. She's growing up so fast, but she's absolutely beautiful, inside and out. Seeing them all happy, healthy, and thriving makes me realize—I must have done something right.

I'm also in a better place. I'm working as a teaching assistant now, something I never imagined for myself, but I love it. I've been off my antidepressants for over a year. That's not to say every day is easy, but I'm managing, and that's what matters. I'm still working on my weight, still chasing my goals, but I'm getting there. My days are filled with work, the gym, and lately, so much of my time has gone into writing this—my story, my truth.

And soon, a new adventure awaits. My partner and I have booked our first holiday abroad—to Portugal. It will be my daughter's first time on a plane, and I just know it's going to be perfect.

For so long, I felt like life was against me, like I was just surviving. But now? Now, I'm living. And that's the biggest victory of all.

And perhaps the most incredible thing happening right now is my partner's decision to officially adopt my daughter and become her dad in every way.

For the past five years, he's raised her as his own. They have a bond like no other—one that has formed so naturally, it's as if they were always meant to be father and daughter. From their silly habits, like randomly burping and making the weirdest noises, to laughing at each other's terrible jokes, they are two peas in a pod. And as strange as it sounds, they even look alike. If you didn't know, you'd never guess they weren't biologically related.

What makes this even more special is that he was someone who never wanted kids—he was so certain that fatherhood wasn't for him. And yet, here he is, stepping up in the most incredible way, proving that love is what makes a family. He treats my boys with the same care and respect, understanding that they already have their dad but still being there as an extra role model for them. But with my daughter, it's different. She has never known anyone else in that role. He has been the one to support her, guide her, and love her unconditionally.

The thought of her having the security of knowing she is his daughter—not just in the way they act, but legally, officially—is something I never imagined, yet it fills my heart in ways I can't explain. She will never have to wonder if she belongs. She will always know that she is loved, that she has two parents who will always be there for her, no matter what.

She is now our daughter. And saying that feels absolutely amazing.

Looking back on everything I've been through, it's almost overwhelming to think about just how much I've had to fight, survive, and push through. My earliest memories weren't filled with warmth and security like they should have been; instead, they were dark, filled with pain, fear, and confusion. Growing up in the system, being bounced from place to place, never truly feeling like I belonged anywhere. The rebelling, lashing out, getting into fights—so many fights—because that was the only way I knew how to cope.

My late teens and early adulthood were no easier. I had to fight my way through, facing one struggle after another. The domestic abuse I endured, the heartache, the constant feeling of trying to find my place in a world that never seemed to want me—all of it shaped me into who I am today. But even in the midst of all that pain, something beautiful had happened. I became a mom. And in those moments, everything changed.

My children became my entire world. They weren't just part of my life—they were my life. They gave me a reason to keep going when I felt like giving up. They gave me the strength I didn't know I had, the fight I didn't realize was in me. No matter what life threw at me, I knew I would fight for them every single day. They were the reason I smiled, even on my darkest days. They are my greatest achievement, my proudest moment, my legacy.

And then, when I least expected it, I met him—my Mr. Right. The man I never thought I'd find, the love I never believed was real. Love, to me, was something that only existed in movies and books, something that wasn't meant for people like me. But he proved me wrong. He showed me that love could be safe, love could be kind, and love could be real. And watching him step up as a dad to our daughter has been one of the most beautiful things I've ever witnessed.

He never wanted kids—he was adamant about that—but life had other plans for him, for us. He embraced fatherhood in a way I never imagined, taking on a role he never thought he'd play. He and our daughter have a bond that is unbreakable. Their silly jokes, their shared mannerisms, even the way they look at each other—it's as if they were always meant to be father and daughter. And now, as he prepares to adopt her officially, my heart feels so full. She will never be without two parents who love her endlessly, and that is everything.

Through all the heartbreak, all the struggles, all the moments I thought I wouldn't make it, I'm still here. And not just surviving—thriving. I have a beautiful family, a man who loves me, and a future that I never thought I'd get to have.

I look back at the girl I used to be—the scared little girl, the angry teenager, the lost young woman—and I wish she could see me now. I wish she could know that she makes it. That all the pain, all the fights, all the nights she cried herself to sleep—it was all leading her here. To happiness. To love. To the life she never thought she deserved.

And if my story proves anything, it's that no matter how dark it gets, there is always light ahead. You just have to keep fighting to reach it.

Printed in Great Britain
by Amazon